Oxford Centre for the Mind

Analytical Thinking

The Oxford Centre for the Mind:

Quick Courses

Gary Lorrison

Analytical Thinking

The Oxford Centre for the Mind

Quick Courses

A guide to the principles of good reasoning and an overview of the ways we get it wrong

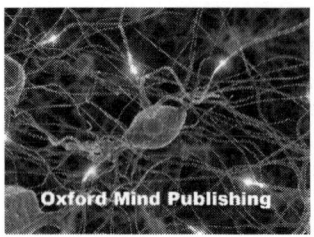

Gary Lorrison

Oxford Mind Publishing

THE OXFORD CENTRE FOR THE MIND LIMITED

#123,
94, London Road
Headington
Oxford OX3 9FN

email: info@oxfordmind.co.uk
web: www.oxfordmind.co.uk

Copyright ©2014 Gary Lorrison

All rights reserved. No portion of this publication may be reproduced, stored in a retrieval system, or transmitted in any form or by any means – electronic, mechanical, photocopy, recording, scanning, or other – except for brief quotations in critical reviews or articles, without the prior written consent of the publisher.

Oxford Mind Publishing is a division of the Oxford Centre for the Mind Limited.

ISBN-13: 978-1499699975

ISBN-10: 1499699972

About the Author

Having studied law at Cambridge, Gary Lorrison started off his career working in London as a solicitor but quickly saw the light and left the legal profession to develop his interest in the mind. He quickly earned two degrees in philosophy but found himself focusing on how one could use the techniques of philosophy, psychology and science to run one's mind more effectively.

Since 2003, he has been actively involved in running personal development training programmes to help people improve their mental performance. He has a special interest in memory training and other ways of helping people absorb information as well as the techniques of logical, critical and analytical thinking and the limits of human rationality.

In his spare time he enjoys walking in the countryside, takes a keen interest in music playing a number of instruments and is an occasional skydiver.

He lives on a farm near Oxford with four dogs, three cats, three ducks, six geese, about five hundred sheep and the occasional human being.

Testimonials

Testimonials for our seminars: -

"Excellent - best course I have been on in ages - thought provoking and insightful"

"Great workshop. Coach created a very relaxing, easy and open atmosphere. Coach was helpful and had a very pleasant way of interacting with us"

"I am very happy I came to this workshop. It was good value for money and provided very useful skills that I know will help my studies"

"It's a great course - I would recommend you go on it"

"Good fun and value for money"

"Do it! - Very interesting and a good approach to de-stressing about work levels etc."

"It really works, especially the visualisation techniques"

For information on all of the courses run by the Oxford Centre for the Mind please visit our website:

www.oxfordmind.co.uk

Contents

1.	Introduction	9
	Part 1	
2.	Argument Construction	13
3.	Prior Conditions	16
4.	The Process of Argumentation	28
5.	Concluding an Argument	37
6.	Reasoning Errors	44
7.	Rhetorical Techniques	58
8.	Psychological Factors	69
9.	Practice Passage	73
	Part 2	
10.	Logical Thinking Problems	80
11.	Endword	93

ONE

INTRODUCTION

Aim

The aim of the Analytical Thinking Course is to improve your logical and critical thinking skills. You will develop your ability to think about real world situations in a logical manner and become aware of certain errors in thinking that you might not previously have been aware of. You will learn how a logical argument is constructed, how to spot errors in reasoning made by others, and about rhetorical and psychological techniques of persuasion that do not rely on proper argument.

Course content

The course is divided into two parts: Analytical Thinking and Logical Thinking Problems. The Analytical Thinking part deals with the real world situations that we have alluded to above. It is divided into the following areas.

- Argument construction (chapters 2 to 5): this section explains what an argument is, what factors are required to construct an argument, valid and invalid forms of reasoning and how conclusions are arrived at.

- Errors in reasoning (chapter 6): this section deals with formal and informal fallacies and other mistakes in reasoning that people often make.

- Rhetorical techniques of persuasion (chapter 7): this section examines techniques used to persuade people to arrive at a particular conclusion that do not rely on the strength of the argument but rather on the way the argument is presented.

Analytical Thinking

- Psychological factors used in argument (chapter 8): this section looks at other factors that may lead us to draw a particular conclusion which again do not rely on the power of the argument being made.

You will find that some of the things that we examine in each of these four areas inevitably overlap to an extent, or alternatively that they belong in more than one category. However, do not concern yourself with that. The important thing is to familiarise yourself thoroughly with all of the various different elements. If you do so, you will find that your reasoning abilities will improve dramatically.

The second part of the course consists of a number of logical problems. These will improve your logical skills by enabling you to use those areas of your brain that process logical thinking. When you have finished these you can continue to practise on your own by going out and buying logical puzzles and games. You will find these in any good book or toy store.

There are other areas of logic, such as symbolic logic or mathematical logic that you are only likely to need to concern yourself with if you are a logician or a mathematician. As such we have not included them within this course.

How to use the course

Each of the four sections within the Analytical Thinking part of the course is further subdivided into different paragraphs which form natural groups that will be apparent when you work through the course. In each paragraph we set out a number of points concerning argumentation, and where appropriate we give examples of how they are used. We suggest that you work through the course and familiarise yourself with each point, making sure that you thoroughly understand it and all of the examples. Also make sure that you are able to recall each element without prompting.

We also suggest that, where we have provided examples, you spend some time trying to make up examples of your own and write them down. By doing so, you will be thinking actively rather than passively.

You can also practise honing your analytical thinking skills by looking at various different real world sources of argument. These might be: -

- The opinion columns of newspapers;

- Non-fiction books containing arguments for or against certain political opinions, such as books written by political commentators;

- TV debating shows;

- Radio commentators.

When reading, watching or listening to these, focus all your energies on identifying the arguments presented and how good the reasoning is. Additionally, pick an area of the course that you have looked at and look out for as many instances of that area as you can. For example, one area we deal with is the assumptions people make, sometimes without realizing it, that underpin their thinking. When you have looked at this section, try to identify as many unstated underlying assumptions as you can.

Also, be sure to complete the Logical Thinking Problems section of the course. This section contains a number of logical puzzles for you to work through (with answers provided). As you work through the problems, make your main task to work out the answer and do not look it up until you either think that you have got it or until you are sure that you cannot go any further. In the latter case, when you have looked at the answer, try to work out why it is right and why you did not get it.

Your secondary task is to observe your thought processes as you solve the problem. For each problem that you do, work out the approach you have adopted and note it down. As you progress, incorporate what you have learnt, so that you have an ever-expanding variety of approaches to use. This should mean that your logical thinking gets more efficient as you progress.

Onword

The following section deals with the process of argumentation. In it you will learn what an argument is, how one is constructed and the factors that come prior to or are necessary for an argument. We then deal with the actual process of reasoning and finally deal with how conclusions are arrived at.

TWO

ARGUMENT CONSTRUCTION

In this section we deal with what goes to make up an argument. Firstly, we set out what an argument is, and equally importantly, what it is not. We then divide the structure of an argument into three parts, which broadly correspond to the following: -

1. What happens before an argument or what is necessary for one to get going;
2. What happens during an argument, the actual process of reasoning;
3. What happens after an argument to bring it to a conclusion.

What is an argument?

An argument is the process of reasoning from one or more premises towards a particular conclusion. If the reasoning used in the argument is valid and sound (these are technical terms which we will explain in due course), then you would have good reasons for agreeing with the person presenting the argument.

A very simple example of an argument is: -

All politicians are liars.
Smith is a politician.
Therefore, Smith is a liar.

You don't have to agree with the first line, but if it were true then the last line would also be true. This can be generalised to the form: -

All As are Bs.
X is an A.
Therefore, X is a B.

Analytical Thinking

A, B and X can be replaced with any proposition you may care to mention.

You may not be presented with all three lines like this though. It is more likely you will see something like the following: -

Smith is a politician: he is clearly a liar.

In this case one of the premises (defined below) has been omitted – you are supposed to know or assume that the truth of the proposition 'all politicians are liars' is so obvious that it is not worth pointing out. Also, the word 'therefore' indicating the conclusion has been omitted, again because it is supposed to be obvious. Sometimes the order may be reversed: -

Smith is a liar because he is a politician.

Here the conclusion comes first and the reason for drawing the conclusion comes afterwards linked by the word 'because'.

We will deal with all of this in more detail, but the point to take in here is than an argument is a very specific way of advancing reasons for a conclusion that you might wish to support.

In contrast, we will not be dealing with what many people may think of as an argument, which is a quarrel. A quarrel is simply a series of assertions and counter-assertions with no reasoning to support them. For instance, the following is not an argument in the sense that we are using: -

"The French are arrogant and smell of garlic."
"That's just not true."
"Of course it is. Everyone knows it."
"I don't. You see I'm French."
"Thought I could smell something."
"Take that!"
BIFF!

Onword

Having outlined what an argument is and what it is not, we will deal with what is necessary in the early stages of an argument.

THREE

PRIOR CONDITIONS

This section deals with elements of argumentation that generally come at the start of the argument, or the underlying assumptions that are in some way psychologically prior to the commencement of the argument.

Premises

A premise is a statement that is needed in order to draw a conclusion (see below for more on Conclusions). It is an essential part of an argument. For instance, in the following line of reasoning, the first two statements are premises: -

Premise 1:   If you go out in the rain, you will get wet.
Premise 2:   You are going out in the rain.
Conclusion: You will get wet.

In this case the premises are stated explicitly. This is not always the case. It is perfectly acceptable for a premise to be taken for granted, perhaps because it is obvious. When this occurs it is called an assumption. There is nothing wrong with making an assumption as long as it is true. For example,

A computer's brain is just like a mouse's brain.
Therefore, the computer is conscious.

The assumption here is that a mouse is conscious. This may be open to dispute. Some would maintain that only humans are truly conscious.

Another word for a suppressed premise like this is an enthymeme. It should be noted that without the truth of this premise the conclusion is a non sequitur (literally it does not follow – i.e. the conclusion does not follow from the premise). Many people are not aware of suppressed premises, so make sure you become aware of them. In the following example, see if you can work out the suppressed premise: -

This TV network makes nothing but rubbish, so you shouldn't watch it.

The suppressed premise is 'if a TV network makes only rubbish, you shouldn't watch it.' The full argument then becomes:

If a TV network makes only rubbish, you shouldn't watch it.
This TV network makes only rubbish.
You shouldn't watch this TV network.

In this case the enthymeme is a matter of opinion and not fact. It is therefore important that you are aware of it, because it may be an opinion with which you do not agree.

Another kind of assumption is the supposition or presupposition. This is an assumption that is made to find out what the world would be like if it were true. The assumption itself need not be true.

For example, a police investigator tracking a criminal might assume that the criminal escaped from a property by jumping out of a window. If that were the case what would he expect to find? Possibly, that there would be marks on the windowsill and the ground below the window would be disturbed.

He can now test the assumption that the criminal escaped through the window by inspecting the windowsill and the ground beneath the window for evidence. If he finds marks on the windowsill and disturbed earth, he has reasons to draw the conclusion that the criminal escaped through the window.

Note that in this case, the investigator must be aware of the possibility of alternative explanations because the reasoning in this case is inductive, and not deductive. Inductive reasoning shows that the explanation is likely to be true, not that it is true. For example, a window cleaner may have visited earlier on in the day.

Evidence

In certain cases, the premises of an argument will be based on evidence of some kind. For instance, in the above example the assumption that criminals who climb out through windows leave marks on a windowsill is based upon evidence. The investigator will know from previous experience that this is what is likely to happen. When an argument is made, it is important to assess the quality of the evidence that is being relied upon. You should distinguish between the following types of evidence.

Empirical evidence

This is evidence based upon experience, research and observation. For example, the proposition, 'the Sun will rise tomorrow' is based upon observations over the totality of human history, that the Sun does indeed rise every day. Suppose the Sun only rose occasionally and at random intervals. In that case, the evidence in support of the proposition would be much weaker (see Inductive Reasoning for more on this).

Empirical evidence is the basis of scientific research. For instance, pharmaceutical companies, conducting trials of new drugs, will test three groups of people. One group will be given the drug under test. The second group will be given no treatment at all, while the third will be given a placebo. A placebo is something that from the point of view of the patient is indistinguishable from the drug in appearance, smell or any other qualities it may have, but which has no clinical effect. The first and third groups will not be told whether they are receiving the drug being tested or the placebo.

If the medical outcomes of the first group, are better than the second and third groups in a sufficiently large number of cases, then that will be taken as evidence that the drug is effective. For the evidence to be taken as good evidence, it must be capable of being duplicated. That is, if another test were carried out, then similar results would have to be obtained. If results could not be duplicated, then that would be evidence that the drug did not work.

The reason that one group is given a placebo is that it has been observed that if people take something that they believe might be effective, then their condition will improve, irrespective of whether it actually is or not. This is due to the power of the mind to alter the state of the body. We discuss this in greater detail in our courses on visualization, concentration & focus and states of mind.

Testimonial Evidence

This is evidence derived from another person who is giving an account of what they themselves have directly observed. It is the kind of evidence that is given in court. Of course testimonial evidence can be true or false and that is why witnesses in court are required to swear to tell the truth. It is also the reason that they are cross-examined by barristers. This examination aims to test whether evidence is true by seeing if the witness is plausible, if they are generally truthful, if the statements they make are consistent with other statements they have made and with the known facts and so on.

Anecdotal evidence

Anecdotal evidence is evidence derived from stories or from other people, often from just a single case. As such it is less strong than empirical evidence. For instance, if someone told you that they had been to see someone who practised crystal healing and as a result they felt better, this would not be very good evidence to suppose that crystal healing is effective. It doesn't mean that crystal healing doesn't work. It may do. It is just that relying on your friend's say so may not be reliable. It ignores the possibility of alternative explanations (such as the placebo effect). Also, to suppose that from one case of healing you can generalise to say something about every case is a rash generalisation. However, if a sufficient number of people said that crystal healing worked for them, it might be a good reason to embark on a scientific enquiry into its effectiveness.

Opinion evidence

Opinion evidence is evidence that is based not on some objective fact about the world, but on what someone thinks about the world. As such it is not necessarily reliable evidence because it is merely what someone thinks.

Above, we gave the example, 'this TV network makes nothing but rubbish'. This is opinion evidence because there is no objective criterion as to what constitutes rubbish on TV.

It can sometimes be difficult to distinguish opinion from fact. For instance, if a jury finds a defendant guilty of murder is it a fact or is it an opinion? Clearly, a jury can be wrong, so the mere fact that a jury has found a defendant guilty does not mean that he in fact committed the crime. How then are you to treat the statement, 'the defendant committed the crime?' Is it fact or mere opinion?

There are some facts that undoubtedly do appear to depend on some form of consensus. For instance, if we suppose that Shakespeare was a great playwright, is it because we all agree that he was, or that there is some fact independent of our views about him that made him great?

Definitions

Arguments are constructed from words, and therefore the meaning of words is crucial to clear argumentation. By the same token, if a word is defined in a way that is different from how you are expecting, or from how it is normally used, then confusion may arise. It is, therefore, important that you are aware of the different ways that words can be defined.

Necessary and sufficient conditions

A necessary condition is a prerequisite, without which it is impossible to fulfil the relevant criterion. For instance, it is a necessary condition to drive legally that a driver possess a valid licence. A necessary condition, therefore, is one that applies to all members of the class.

A sufficient condition is one that if fulfilled, guarantees success. Sufficient conditions for being a competent driver might be knowing which pedals to press, how far and in which direction to turn the steering wheel, the rules of the road and so on. Possessing a licence would not be a sufficient condition for being a competent driver because it is possible to be a competent driver without a licence, and also to be a poor driver and still possess a licence.

How does this relate to definitions? One way of looking at definitions is in terms of necessary and sufficient conditions. For example, consider what it takes to define a painting as a work of art. It would seem to be a necessary condition that it is an object with paint on it. However, this is not a sufficient condition, because not all painting is art. For instance, you would not consider a painted house-front a work of art. Sufficient conditions might be being subject to critical acclaim, being sold in a gallery, or simply being painted by an artist (although this last example may be subject to the criticism that it is a circular definition – see below).

Family resemblance terms

Some concepts do not appear to be definable in terms of necessary and sufficient conditions. An example of this is the word 'game'. It is supposedly impossible to find some feature that is common to all games (a necessary condition) or which if fulfilled guarantees that it is a game (a sufficient condition). For instance, it might be supposed that two players are necessary for a game. Yet some card games, such as patience, can be played alone. Or it might be argued that an element of competition might guarantee that an activity is a game. However, this, if true, would make capitalist economic activity – and war – into games. Instead, we can define what a game is in terms of common features and overlapping resemblances (the use of family resemblance terms is a counter to the Socratic Fallacy – see below).

Stipulative definitions

In certain circumstances, the person using a word or phrase may want to use it in a way that leaves no room for doubt in order to avoid any confusion. To do this he may specify exactly how the word is to be understood when he is using it. For example, a person writing about intelligence may define being intelligent as having an IQ of above 100, which is the average IQ. However, this may differ from what most people think of as being intelligent. Presumably, most people would require an intelligent person to have an IQ significantly higher than the average. Because of the dichotomy between the two, it is important to be aware when a stipulative definition is being used, otherwise confusion may arise

Another thing to be aware of is so called 'humpty-dumptying', taken from the Humpty Dumpty character created by Lewis Carroll. Humpty-dumptying is the practice of giving words a private meaning and is an extreme form of stipulative definition. Humpty Dumpty said that the word 'glory' meant whatever he wanted it to mean, no more no less. However, the danger here is that no one else will understand or agree with the meaning of the word.

Dictionary definition

A dictionary definition purports to be an account of how a word is used and as such can be a good first port of call for seeing what a word actually means. However, a dictionary is just a book written by a certain group of people and they are capable of making mistakes just like everyone else. They may define a word in a way which is different from how most people use it. Furthermore, a particular word's definition may differ from dictionary to dictionary, may be short, may be vague, and may be defined in terms of synonyms. For instance, a dictionary may define 'musician' as 'someone who makes music'. Unless you know what music is, this is not much help.

Circular definition

A circular definition is a definition that does nothing to advance your knowledge because what it is that you are trying to define occurs in the definition. In the example above concerning musician, if you were then to look up 'music' in the dictionary and find that it said, 'that which is made by a musician', it would not advance your knowledge very much. For you to learn anything, music would have to be defined by independent criteria.

Ultimately all dictionary definitions are circular because all the words in a dictionary are defined using words that are also defined in the dictionary. You need to understand some of the words independently in order to use a dictionary at all. If you think about this for a moment it is obvious, otherwise you would be able to learn a language simply by reading a dictionary.

Meaning

In addition to knowing that words may be defined in different ways, it is also important to note that their meaning may not always be obvious. In the following examples, we set out the different ways confusion may arise. Being aware of this you can eliminate poor usage from your own language, and spot when others are using language in ways that might lead to confusion.

Ambiguity

Ambiguity arises when what is said can be understood in more than one way, leading to possible confusion. There are three types of ambiguity: -

1   Lexical ambiguity

This occurs where a word has greater than one meaning, and can therefore be understood in more than one way. For instance, 'the legendary King Arthur' could be taken to mean that King Arthur was particularly famous, or alternatively that he was not real.

2   Referential ambiguity

This occurs when a word may refer to more than one thing, and it is not clear which thing it is referring to. It particularly occurs when we use pronouns like him, her, or them. For instance, 'David took out a gun and told John to lie on the ground. Sarah said to him, "don't do anything stupid"'. In this case, it is not clear whether Sarah is talking to David or John and more information is required. Referential ambiguities can be eliminated by specifying who is being referred to. Sometimes it may be obvious from the context. For example, if Sarah had said, 'don't do anything stupid with that gun', it would have been clear that she was talking to David.

3   Syntactical ambiguity (or amphiboly)

This occurs when the word order of an expression is open to two interpretations. For example, the phrase, 'a small bone eating demon', could mean a small demon that eats bones, or a demon that eats small bones. Syntactical ambiguity can be eliminated by changing the word order, as we have done here. Alternatively, hyphens can be used as clarification by connecting the relevant concepts. Thus, we can clarify the phrase so that it becomes, 'small bone-eating demon' i.e. a small demon that eats bones.

Equivocation

This is related to lexical ambiguity. Equivocation happens where the same word is used twice in a phrase using two different meanings. For example, 'legends are not true, but Elvis is a legend'. It invites the conclusion that Elvis did not exist, which of course is false.

Some / all confusion

This occurs when the words some or all are omitted. For instance, consider the phrase 'politicians are liars'. Does it mean that some politicians are liars, or that all are? Without more it is not clear.

Vagueness

This happens where there is a lack of precision in the expression that is being used. For example, what does it take for someone to be bald? Is it a complete absence of hair on the head? Presumably not, otherwise we could not say that Homer Simpson is bald because he has three hairs on his head. However, there is not an exact number of hairs that distinguishes someone who is bald from someone who is not. Sometimes, the same phrase may be vague in one context and sufficiently precise in another. For instance, if you were asked your age and you said over thirty, this may be precise enough in some circumstances. It may make you ineligible for a job as a model for example. If you were, say, applying for a bank loan, the bank may require your exact date of birth.

Imply / infer confusion

People often confuse these two words, but they are essentially opposite in meaning. An implication occurs when premises lead to a conclusion. For example, 'the fact that Iraqi scientists were buying uranium implies that they were interested in making nuclear weapons.' The use of 'infer' here would be wrong. However, it would be correct to say, 'from the fact that Iraq is buying uranium, we can infer that Iraq is building nuclear weapons'. In other words, an inference is a conclusion that is drawn by a particular person or party.

Pedantry

In the examples of meaning we have given so far, we have identified examples which result in confusion because they rely on some form of inaccuracy. Pedantry differs in that it is over-concerned with accuracy. Pedantry happens when one is obsessed with detail, and accordingly misses the point. For example, suppose a sign says, 'please don't walk on the grass'. A pedant might argue that he is allowed to run across the grass or jump on the grass. It can be difficult to argue with a pedant, because in a sense they are right. The important thing to realise is that they are missing the point about what is important.

Theorising

Theorising is something that we all do, despite its scientific connotations. It occurs when we imagine how the world might be, to find out what would happen if that were the case. A theory is a set of statements about how the world may (or may not) be. It is not necessarily true, although it might be. A good scientific theory should be capable of explaining why a situation is like it is, make predictions as to how the situation will change in the future, and should be capable of being falsified, so that we have a criteria for judging whether it is right or wrong.

Hypothesis

A hypothesis is a little like an assumption and comes prior to a theory. It is an assumption about how a situation might be and is subject to confirmation by empirical evidence, or alternatively to refutation by counter-example. For example, a social scientist may advance the hypothesis that crime is determined by the level of poverty in a society. She may give examples of how poor neighbourhoods have lots of crime while wealthy ones have little crime.

This hypothesis would be undermined if one could identify neighbourhoods which were very poor but had low levels of crime, or neighbourhoods which were rich and had high crime levels. If this evidence came to light, the scientist would have to discard that hypothesis and try to come up with a new one. She may say that poverty is one of the factors that determine the level of crime and that there may be others. If, however, no counter examples could be found then the hypothesis may acquire the status of a theory.

Experiments and thought experiments

We use experiments and thought experiments to test a hypothesis. For instance, we might think that a car would brake more effectively with carbon-fibre brakes rather than disc brakes. To find out whether this is so, we could conduct an experiment to compare the braking distances in cars with the two different types of brake, to see which worked better.

We might conduct a thought experiment to test ideas that cannot be tested by actual experiment. For example, we might suppose that people should only be criminally responsible for consequences that they actually intend. You might then conduct the following thought experiment. Imagine a person who puts a blindfold on and goes out into a street firing a gun randomly but not intending to kill anyone? Should he be responsible for any deaths or injuries he causes?

Adopting the hypothesis that he should only be held responsible for what he intends, then he is not. But most people would think that he should be morally responsible for the deaths and injuries he has caused, and so the hypothesis is undermined.

Conditional statements

A conditional statement is a statement of the form, if P then Q. For example, 'if you don't slow down, we will crash', or, 'if John had never met Paul, the Beatles would never have existed'. They purport to say something about how the world is or might be, and what this would imply if it were so.

Onword

This concludes our examination of the elements that are prior to an argument. In the following section, we concern ourselves with the actual processes of reasoning.

FOUR

THE PROCESS OF ARGUMENTATION

In the previous section we discussed some of the conditions that are necessary for an argument to be conducted, and some other related factors. In this section, we look at the process of reasoning itself. There are two types of reasoning, deductive and inductive. We will deal with deductive reasoning first. Deductive reasoning occurs in cases where the truth of the premises guarantees the truth of the conclusion, providing the form of the argument is correct.

Deductive reasoning

Deductive reasoning is reasoning of the following form: -

1. All men are mortal.
   Socrates is a man.
   Therefore, Socrates is mortal.

2. All men are mortal.
   Socrates is not mortal.
   Therefore, Socrates is not a man.

3. All men are fish.
   Socrates is a man.
   Therefore, Socrates is a fish.

4. If you work too hard you will get ill.
   You are ill.
   Therefore, you have worked too hard.

5. If you work too hard you will get ill.
   You have not worked too hard.

Therefore, you are not ill.

These are all forms of deductive reasoning. However, which ones would you agree with? Look at each one closely and decide which ones you think are right.

You have good reasons to believe (1) only. Why is this so? Only (1) is an example of sound and valid deductive reasoning. Both premises are true and the conclusion follows from the premises.

(2) and (3) are examples of valid reasoning, but are not sound. You could agree with the conclusion only if you were happy to agree with the premises. However the premises are false. In (2) the premise 'Socrates is not mortal' is false. In (3) the premise 'all men are fish' is false.

(4) and (5) are examples of invalid reasoning because the form or structure of the argument is wrong. If you agreed with the conclusion in these cases your powers of reasoning are defective.

We examine these distinctions in more detail below.

Valid reasoning

Valid reasoning is reasoning that is truth preserving from premises to conclusion. That is, if the premises are true then the conclusion must necessarily be true. In the above examples (1), (2), and (3) all fulfil this condition. Look at these again and see if you understand why. As we have already stated, the fact that the reasoning is valid does not make the conclusion true – merely that if the premises were true, then the conclusion would be.

Another example of valid reasoning is,

If anyone commits murder, they should go to jail.
You have committed murder.
So you should go to jail.

Examples (4) and (5) above are examples of invalid reasoning. Another example of invalid reasoning is,

If anyone commits murder, they should go to jail.
You are in jail.
Therefore you have committed murder.

To learn how to distinguish valid from invalid reasoning, it is helpful to learn a little terminology. The antecedent is the first part of an if...then statement, and the consequent is the second part, so in the above statement,

… anyone commits murder…

is the antecedent. The consequent is the second part, the part which comes after 'then' (in this case the word then has been omitted but is implied). So, here, the consequent is,

…they should go to jail

You should note that the example 'all men are mortal', can be rearranged to become 'if you are a man, then you are mortal'. So, 'you are a man' corresponds to the antecedent, while, 'you are mortal' corresponds to the consequent. This can be generalised, so that all statements of the form All X's are Y's can become, 'if you are an X then you are a Y'. (Here X and Y are any proposition you may care to make).

To reason validly, you can affirm the antecedent or deny the consequent. An affirmation or denial is what is contained in the second line of each of the examples, so in,

All men are mortal.
Socrates is a man.
Therefore Socrates is mortal.

'Socrates is a man' is an affirmation. It is an affirmation because it is a positive proposition. A denial is a negative proposition. So 'Socrates is not a man' is a denial.

Affirming the antecedent

Affirming the antecedent is a form of valid reasoning, and is of the general form,

If P then Q.
P.
Therefore, Q.

P and Q can be any proposition you care to mention. So, the following are examples of valid reasoning, affirming the antecedent.

If you are a doctor then you have been to medical school.
You are a doctor.
Therefore, you have been to medical school.

If you are a goldfish you can ride a bike.
You are a goldfish.
Therefore, you can ride bike.

This latter example shows again that an argument can be valid in spite of its absurdity.

Denying the consequent

Denying the consequent is another form of valid reasoning. If the premises are true then the conclusion is true, and is of the general form,

If P then Q.
Not Q.
Therefore, not P.

Examples of this form are,

If an aircraft's wings fall off, then it will fall out of the sky.
No aircraft have fallen from the sky.
Therefore no aircrafts' wings have fallen off.

If your car runs out of fuel, then it will come to a halt.
Your car has not come to a halt.
Therefore your car has not run out of fuel.

These arguments remain valid even if the premises are false. For instance, in the above example you might take issue with the statement if your car runs out of fuel, then it will come to a halt. There may be circumstances where it is not true, for example, if you are on a downhill slope or driving over a cliff. However, the point is that if it were true, then the conclusion would be true. And, of course, this particular statement is likely to be true (see inductive reasoning below).

Invalid reasoning

Invalid reasoning is to be avoided. It is reasoning that is not truth preserving from premises to conclusion. That is, if the premises are true then the conclusion is not necessarily true. It either might be true or it might be false, depending on the circumstances. In the examples at the start of this section, (4) and (5) fulfil this condition. Denying the antecedent and affirming the consequent are both examples of invalid reasoning.

Denying the antecedent

Denying the antecedent is a formal fallacy. A formal fallacy is one which relates to the form of an argument, not its content. It takes the form,

If P then Q.
Not P.
Therefore, not Q.

Examples are,

If you have the winning lottery ticket, then you are rich.
You don't have the winning lottery ticket.
Therefore you are not rich.

If you listen to the radio, then you'll be aware of what music is new.
You don't listen to the radio.
Therefore, you are not aware of new music.

The reason that these arguments are not valid is that in both cases there are potentially alternative explanations. In the first case, you might be very highly paid, or have inherited a lot of money or any number of other explanations. In the second, you might work in a nightclub, or in a music shop, or play in a band.

In these cases, the conclusion does not follow from the premises. It is a *non sequitur*.

Affirming the consequent

Affirming the consequent is another formal fallacy and takes the general form,

If P then Q.
Q.
Therefore, P.

Examples are,

If you run around naked you will get cold.
You are cold.
Therefore you have been running around naked.

The problem with both cases of invalid reasoning is that the conclusion may or may not be true. The conclusions ignore the possibility of alternative explanations, and treats the 'if' in the first line, as meaning if and only if. So,

If and only if you run around naked, you will get cold.
You are cold.
Therefore you have been running around naked.

This form of reasoning is now valid, although the first premise is clearly incorrect.

We have now distinguished between forms of valid and invalid deductive reasoning. There is one more distinction that you should be aware of and that is between a sound and unsound argument. We have used both in the above examples.

Sound and unsound arguments

A sound argument is a valid argument that contains true premises and which therefore guarantees a true conclusion. An example is,

All bachelors are not married.
I am a bachelor.
Therefore, I am not married.

An unsound argument is one in which the conclusion is not true. It is possible for an argument to be valid but not sound. For example,

All pink elephants can fly.
I am a pink elephant.
Therefore, I can fly.

This is a valid argument, but it is not sound (and clearly absurd!)

Inductive arguments

An inductive argument differs from a deductive argument in that true premises provide good reasons for believing the conclusion, but they do not guarantee its truth. Inductive arguments are the stuff of empirical evidence. Almost any conclusion that we draw concerning the real world is likely to be provisional to some degree, even those things that we unthinkingly take for granted have the potential to surprise us.

For example, you might have observed a large number of sheep and concluded, 'all sheep are white'. You might have good reasons for believing this if you have observed a very large number of sheep, but, of course, there are black sheep. So you would have drawn a false conclusion.

Adopting the form we have used for deductive arguments, an inductive argument might run as follows,

All the sheep I have ever seen are white.
The animal in the shed is a sheep.
Therefore, the animal in the shed is white.

This conclusion, while likely to be true, may be false.

Analogies

Inductive arguments are based on analogies, that is, the idea that one thing is like another. In the above case, the analogy was that the unknown sheep was like the previously observed sheep in its relevant aspect: its colour. When making analogies, it is important to make sure that the analogy is relevant. One famous analogy is used to argue for the existence is God. It runs as follows: -

Objects such as computers are very complicated and could not have arisen without a designer.

Human beings are just as complicated as computers and must therefore have a designer, i.e. God.

However, it may be that there are sufficient differences between the two cases to undermine the argument. For instance, in evolutionary theory, the complexity of the human organism is explained by tiny changes from generation to generation over billions of years, subject to the forces of natural selection.

Another example is an argument for outlawing alcoholic drinks. For example, consider this argument: 'alcoholic drinks are ingested substances that adversely affect your state of health and your mind. Crack-cocaine is also an ingested substance that adversely affects your health and your mind. If crack-cocaine is illegal, then alcoholic drinks should be illegal'. A counter to this argument is that the analogy is not relevant, because the adverse health consequences of taking crack-cocaine are much greater than of drinking alcohol.

You might use a similar argument for taking cannabis. You might say that both alcohol and cannabis have mild adverse health effects, but they also provide you with a benefit in that they make you feel happier and more relaxed. However, again, the analogy is not necessarily a good one. One important difference is that alcohol is legal whereas cannabis is illegal. Whether you take cannabis on that basis will depend on how much weight you give to obeying the law.

However, if you were a lawmaker considering whether to legalise cannabis, the mere fact that cannabis is illegal and alcohol legal is not a relevant distinction. In order to justify maintaining the illegality of cannabis, it would be necessary to find another relevant distinction. For example, you might argue that taking cannabis inevitably leads you on to take hard drugs. In fact, many lawmakers make this argument and make the mistake of affirming the consequent. Thus: -

All people that take hard drugs have taken cannabis.
You take cannabis.
Therefore, you will move on to take hard drugs.

That this is invalid can be shown by adopting another argument of exactly the same form: -

All people that take hard drugs have drunk water at some time.
You are drinking water.
Therefore you will take hard drugs.

Onword

This concludes the section on the reasoning process. In the next section we will deal with how conclusions are arrived at, how they might be supported and how they can be undermined.

FIVE

CONCLUDING AN ARGUMENT

The conclusion is the judgment that the line of reasoning in a particular argument invites you to draw. In the arguments we have set out previously the conclusion has been the third of the three lines: -

All men are mortal.
Socrates is a man.
Therefore, Socrates is mortal.

The conclusion here is, 'Socrates is mortal'. However, in normal conversation the conclusion does not necessarily come at the end. For example, in the phrase, 'this government should be voted out because they have ruined the economy', the conclusion - that the government should be voted out - comes first.

Multiple conclusions

In certain situations there may be more than one conclusion that is capable of being drawn. Suppose that you have a daily newspaper delivery, but for one week only it fails to get delivered and then delivery is resumed. Which of the following conclusions would you draw?

1. The delivery boy went on vacation and the shopkeeper forgot to find a replacement.

2. The delivery boy was murdered, and it took the shop a few days to find a replacement.

3. Aliens were observing your house and, wanting to know what was going on in the world, stole your newspaper before you had a chance to get to it. Then after a week they returned to their own planet.

Hopefully, you would draw the first conclusion. The second might be true. The third could conceivably be true (at least in Hollywood). So how do we decide which conclusion is the right one? Generally, the correct approach is to apply what is known as 'Ockham's razor', which states that the simplest explanation is usually the best. That means the conclusion that needs the fewest and simplest assumptions to back it up. In this case, it is the first conclusion. If you were inclined to go for the third conclusion you would probably be guilty of wishful thinking.

Acceptance and rejection of arguments

When you are engaged in an argument, you may want others to accept the argument you are advancing, or reject a conclusion that someone else is inviting you to draw. Sometimes, the reasoning being advanced may seem to be sound but the conclusion, bizarre. On other occasions, the conclusion, while sound, may have other implications that you might not want to accept. We deal with these situations below.

Refutation

A refutation is proof that a conclusion you are being invited to draw is untrue. For instance, if someone said, 'there have been no great women scientists', you could use the example of Marie Curie as a refutation. A refutation should be contrasted with a repudiation, which is a mere denial that the argument being advanced is true.

One form of a refutation is a knock down argument. This is an argument that completely refutes the argument being advanced. In the above example, citing Marie Curie as a great scientist would be a knock down argument, because it would be inconsistent to believe that Marie Curie was a great scientist and that there have not been any great female scientists. To maintain the position one would have to argue that Marie Curie was not a great scientist.

Contradictions and contraries

The knock down argument identified relies on a form of contradiction. A contradiction occurs when there are two statements that are mutually incompatible. It would be inconsistent to believe both of them. For example, if you say, 'I have been to New York' and then, 'I have never been to New York', at least one statement must be false. Of course, these statements may both be true at different times. If you have never been to New York before, you can truthfully say that you have never been to New York. If you subsequently visit New York later on in your life, you can then truthfully say that you have been to New York. However, you cannot ever truthfully say again that you have never been to New York.

Note that there is a distinction between contradictions and contraries. Contraries are statements that cannot both be true but both can be false. For example, the statements, 'milk is the best health drink' and 'orange juice is the best health drink' are contraries. Clearly, if one is true than the other is not. However, it might be the case that neither is and that some other drink is the best health drink.

Absurd consequences and biting the bullet

Another way of showing that an argument is false is by showing that it would lead to absurd consequences if it were true. For example, if someone were to say that anyone who has taken cannabis should be locked up for life, and you were to show that half the population had taken cannabis at some time in their life, then it would mean that half the population would have to be locked up, which is clearly ludicrous.

A possible response to the absurd consequences move is to bite the bullet and accept those consequences. In the above example, you might say that if it did indeed mean locking up half the population for life, then that is what should be done, even if it does seem mad.

Suppose we argue that the main aim of government policy is to maximise happiness across the population as a whole. Evidence might then be adduced to show that happiness could be maximised by imprisoning one innocent man for a crime he didn't commit. For example, suppose a horrible crime had been committed, and the tabloid press are pressing for a conviction, any conviction. Also, suppose that they cause their readers to believe that a particular person is guilty of the crime. Then it might be the case that the increase in happiness on the part of the mob and the victim's family, police and so on, as a result of his conviction would outweigh the increase in unhappiness on the part of the wrongly condemned man.

If this were the case, then this would appear to be a refutation of the argument that the sole aim of government policy should be to maximise happiness because under these circumstances the government would be committed to the conviction and imprisonment of an innocent man.

Most people would find this entirely unacceptable because they believe that it is wrong to lock up innocent people. However, a person committed to the other viewpoint might bite the bullet and accept that under certain circumstances it is acceptable to lock up the innocent. Totalitarian governments often do this and presumably rely on a justification that is similar to this.

In such a fundamental case of disagreement, it is unlikely that the argument could be taken any further.

Inconsistency, companions in guilt, hypocrisy and playing Devil's advocate

It may be the case that an argument also has consequences beyond those that the person making the argument might have anticipated. For instance, someone who is opposed to boxing may argue that it should be banned because some boxers have suffered brain damage and died. However, if the reason for banning a sport is that it can cause injury and death, then any number of sports should be banned, including rugby, motor-racing, skydiving, snorkelling, horse-riding and so on. People have suffered injury and died in all those sports as well.

If the advocate of the ban on boxing is to avoid the charge of inconsistency, then he should propose banning these sports, too. To avoid this, he may then attempt to show how boxing is different from those other sports. However, there is a danger that he may end up appearing to make *ad hoc* arguments to justify his position.

Another way of exposing inconsistency is to show that the argument has implications for the advocate as well. This move is called a companions in guilt move.

For example, if a politician is advocating compulsory drug tests for persons in positions of authority, then he must accept that he should be prepared to undergo them as well. If he refuses, then he may be guilty of *hypocrisy*.

Hypocrisy is where a person advocates one position but practises another that is inconsistent with it. A politician who advocates compulsory state education for all children, but sends his own child to a private school is guilty of hypocrisy.

Note that this is a kind of *ad hominem* attack. That is, an argument which addresses the proponent of the argument and not its substance. Just because the proponent is a hypocrite does not mean that he is necessarily wrong. So it may be that compulsory state education is right despite the politician's hypocrisy.

Hypocrisy is not to be confused with playing *Devil's advocate*. This is where a person advocates the case against a particular argument, not because he believes in what he is saying, but because he wants to test the strength of the case against it, examining it for flaws and loopholes. So if someone believes in capital punishment, he might play Devil's advocate by putting the strongest case against capital punishment that he can think of. If the reasons for capital punishment stand up against his assault, then the case for it is strengthened.

Ad hoc reasoning

Ad hoc reasoning occurs when an arbitrary assumption is added to a hypothesis purely in order to make it fit the facts. This might be done when a hypothesis explains what is happening, fits the facts and makes good predictions, except for one observation that consistently fails to agree with it.

For instance, a botanist might advance the hypothesis no animal can live for over 150 years because no animal has ever been discovered that does. Then it is discovered that some giant tortoises do live for more than 150 years. Rather than abandon his hypothesis, he may instead amend it so that

Analytical Thinking

it becomes, no animal can live for 150 years, except for the giant tortoise. This is acceptable, but, if a number of other species are subsequently discovered that also live for more than 150 years, it would undermine the hypothesis, because it would require the addition of an arbitrary number of ad hoc clauses, and one of the reasons for advocating a hypothesis is to explain what is happening and why. A hypothesis that has a large number of ad hoc clauses fails to do this.

Paradoxes

Paradoxes are interesting because they are conclusions that appear to be based on impeccable reasoning from uncontroversial premises, and yet they lead to conclusions that are clearly wrong.

An example is the Sorites Paradox: if you put a large amount of grains of salt on the ground you will have a heap. If you remove one grain, then you will still have a heap. Now remove another, and another, and so on. At some point, you will eventually have only one grain left and one grain is clearly not a heap. It must then be the case that at some point removing one grain brings the heap to an end. This would seem to be contrary to the intuitions that the addition or removal of a mere one grain cannot make or destroy a heap. This is the paradox.

Another example of a paradox is the Paradox of the Unexpected Test. In this, a student is told that the following week he will be given a test, but he will not know which day he is going to receive it.

The student argues as follows, 'If I reach Thursday night, and have not had the test, then I will know it is going to be on Friday. But then I will know which day the test is going to be on, so the test cannot be on Friday'.

Then he goes on to reason, 'Now, if I reach Wednesday night and have not had the test, I already know that it cannot be on Friday, and by the same token, it cannot be on Thursday, because then I would know which day it is going to be on, so it cannot be on Thursday'.

Using the same reasoning he goes on to eliminate the possibility of the test being on Wednesday, then Tuesday, then Monday. He has now eliminated the possibility of the test being given on any day of the week. This runs counter to a very strong intuition that it is possible to give a test on an unexpected day. Something would appear to be wrong.

Paradoxes force us to examine our reasoning or to revise our assumptions because they show that our intuitions about logical reasoning and the state of the world may be inconsistent. They challenge us to think deeply about the situation to ascertain what the root of the problem is, not always successfully. The Sorites paradox dates from Ancient Greece, and has yet to be adequately resolved.

Onword

This concludes the section on argument structure. We have explained what an argument purports to do, and the different stages that make up an argument. In the next section, we will examine some common reasoning errors, known as fallacies and other forms of bad argument.

SIX
REASONING ERRORS

Reasoning Errors

In this section we examine reasoning errors, known as fallacies, and other forms of poor reasoning. We have already encountered some reasoning errors in our examination of valid and invalid arguments. These are known as formal fallacies – because they rely on the *form* of the argument. Other fallacies are known as informal fallacies.

Formal fallacies

We have already outlined a number of formal fallacies. A formal fallacy is where the premises are true but the conclusion is not necessarily true (i.e. the argument is not truth preserving), and is so called because it depends on the *form* of the argument. The conclusion may be true, but even so, it is not arrived at by any reliable method.

For example, the premises:

All As are Fs.
All Bs are Fs.

May lead you to draw the conclusion:

All As are Bs.

However, a moment's reflection reveals that this is not correct. For example, substituting apples for A, bananas for B, and fruit for F we get:

All apples are fruits.
All bananas are fruits.

Both of these are true premises, but the conclusion,

All apples are bananas.

does not follow. It is a *non sequitur*.

Another example of a formal fallacy leading to a *non sequitur* is the following: -

All witches have black cats.
My neighbour has a black cat.
Therefore my neighbour is a witch.

The conclusion, while wrong, is at least understandable. A non sequitur can be even more bizarre though. For example,

It is raining outside today.
Therefore, the Olympics will take place in Brazil!

In this case, the conclusion has no relation at all to the premise. It would be mad to draw such a conclusion, despite the fact that it is true.

Bad reasons fallacy

This is another example of a formal fallacy, again based on the structure of the argument. In this case, a true conclusion can be arrived at from false premises: -

All birds have two legs.
The President is a bird.
Therefore, the President has two legs.

The conclusion, while true, is a *non sequitur*.

Informal fallacies

All fallacies that are not formal fallacies are informal fallacies. These are fallacies that are not strictly related to the form of the argument, but rather to its content. We identify a number below: -

Genetic fallacy

This is an argument based on the belief, '*if X originated from Y, then X must have certain features in common with Y*'. That is, the belief that because one thing comes from another it must share certain important features. But this is not necessarily the case. For example, chickens come from eggs, but don't share any important features with eggs. They don't crack when dropped and cannot easily be scrambled.

Etymological fallacy

This occurs when an advocate assumes that the original meaning of a word fixes the meaning for all time. But, of course, words can change their meaning over time. For instance, *classical music* used to mean music that was made in the Classical period as opposed to the Baroque, Romantic or Modern periods. Now, however, classical music means orchestral or chamber music played on the instruments traditionally associated with an orchestra. For the best current meaning of a word or phrase it is probably best to refer to a dictionary, but remember always to treat the dictionary definition with a degree of scepticism.

Value judgment fallacy

This is a point that people often make in response to opinions on works of art, for example. If A were to say, '*the Mona Lisa is a great painting*', it would be wrong for B to say in response, '*that's a value judgment*' in an attempt to show that the Mona Lisa was not a great painting. Value judgments can be both good and bad, and what B presumably meant was, '*that's a poor value judgment. The Mona Lisa is not a good painting*'. The onus is then on him to say why that is the case.

Gambler's fallacy

This is a common fallacy among gamblers, and it is the belief that the longer you are on a losing streak, the greater your chances of winning on the next bet. For example, suppose that you have tossed a coin ten times, you have called it heads every time and it has always landed tails up.

You might believe that the chances of it coming up heads the next time increase, because you believe that your luck must change some time (a case of *wishful thinking*). This is clearly wrong, because the coin does not know what you are calling and has no memory of what it has done in the past. In some circumstances the converse may even be true. If a coin kept coming up tails, it may be more reasonable to assume that it is not a fair coin.

Van Gogh fallacy

This is an unreliable argument of the form,

Van Gogh was a poor artist while he was alive, but is now recognised as a great artist.
I am a poor artist.
Therefore, I will be recognised as a great artist.

This argument makes the mistake of assuming that the quality two parties have in common is the cause of the other, desired, quality. In this case, it is assumed that poverty, a quality I share with Van Gogh, is the cause of greatness as an artist. In fact, it is more likely to be the quality of the paintings he produced, combined with trends in public taste and numerous other factors, that contributed to his greatness as an artist.

Circularity

A circular argument is an argument of the form *A happens because of B*, and then proceeds to justify B happening because A has happened.

An example of a circular argument is,

God exists because the Bible says he exists

The Bible's reliability is then justified by saying,

The Bible is the word of God.

Analytical Thinking

This argument is not likely to convince anyone who does not already believe in the existence of God. What is required is independent evidence as to the existence of God. If there is no such independent evidence, then the argument is *viciously circular*.

Another kind of circularity is known as *begging the question*. This happens in an argument when you assume the point under discussion has already been decided. For example, if in a trial for murder the accused person were referred to as the murderer, this would be begging the question. It assumes that he is the murderer when this is the question to be determined.

A concept closely related to begging the question is the *complex question*, the paradigm example being the question, '*when did you stop beating your wife?*' Clearly, the problem with complex questions is that they assume facts that have not been determined. The solution is to draw out the assumption by asking *what leads you to believe that...*

Yet another form of circularity is the *Catch 22 situation*, based on the novel by Joseph Heller. In his book, which is set in wartime, the only way a pilot could get out of flying was to be grounded by showing that he was mad. Yet, given the dangers of flying anyone wanting to be grounded must surely be sane, while anyone wanting to fly must be mad. So if you wanted to get out of flying, you couldn't, but if you didn't want to you could!

A variation on this is the following you sometimes see on signs in offices: -

1   *The boss is always right.*
2   *If the boss is wrong, see Rule 1.*

Fallacies concerning consensus

Some arguments rely on the notion that if enough people believe an idea, it becomes true. This can be the case in certain limited sets of circumstance, for instance when dealing with public taste, but certain facts are true independently of what people think.

The democratic fallacy

This is notion that a majority of opinion can reliably be a guide as to the correct way to act. In certain circumstances it may be. For example, if we wanted to decide whether certain acts of sex or violence should not be shown on television due to the concern that they might be offensive, then it would be acceptable to see whether a majority were actually offended by such material. However, in certain circumstances, it would not be appropriate. It would not be appropriate to take a vote on which is the best method for treating illnesses such as cancer and heart disease. Instead, it is best to leave this to a medical expert.

Truth by consensus

This is an allied notion that a statement can be taken as true because it is agreed upon by the majority (or even everybody). In the ancient world it was generally believed that the Earth was flat, and the centre of the universe. That didn't make it true. This raises an interesting question about the sources of our knowledge. Presumably as you read this you believe that the Earth is a sphere and that it orbits the Sun. What reasons do you have for believing that? Are they good reasons?

Sometimes, truth can be revealed by consensus. If everyone agrees that the Beatles are the most popular pop group in history then that would seem to make it true. It would cease to be true if everyone decided that the Rolling Stones were instead. A counter to this might be to define popularity by record sales. If so, the Beatles would still be the most popular group, by virtue of having sold more records. However, that would require a *stipulative definition* of popularity.

Generalisations

A generalisation is when we say that because something is true in some cases then it must be true in all cases. It is the basis of *inductive reasoning* and therefore not an error in itself. It may be appropriate in some instances, but it should always be remembered that just because something is true in some cases it does not necessarily mean that it is always true. If we have a sufficiently large number of examples it may be appropriate to make the generalisation. If we had observed a large number of a particular species of bird and found that they all flew south in winter, then we might be justified in supposing that all birds of that species did so. Since a generalisation purports to apply to *all* cases under discussion, it can be shown to be false by just one counterexample. (See below for further discussion on counterexamples).

Rash generalisations

This type of generalisation is to be avoided. It is a generalised statement based on insufficient evidence. For example, it is a rash generalisation to suppose that because some rock groups can neither sing nor play their instruments, that no rock is capable of singing or playing their instruments. Of course, there are some talented rock singers and instrumentalists about.

Provincialism

This is another form of unacceptable generalisation, and assumes that the only correct way to behave is the way people behave in your peer group or locale. Some people might assume that because a particular form of government is appropriate for them, then it is appropriate for other countries (and it is often a short step from this to imposing it on other countries). Or because a particular practice is unacceptable in one culture (for example, eating horseflesh), it is assumed to be generally unacceptable, when in fact it may be completely acceptable in other cultures. Provincial thinking like this can be the basis for intolerance and racism.

Counterexamples

Since a generalisation purports to say something about *all* cases, then it can be refuted by just one counterexample. We have already seen that the proposition that there have been no great women scientists can be refuted by citing Marie Curie. That is all it takes.

In this context note the common expression '*the exception that proves the rule*'. This seems to state that a counterexample somehow provides evidence in favour of the rule.

In fact, any counterexample at all serves to undermine the rule as we have just seen. The saying therefore doesn't seem to make sense and the reason for this is due to a change in the meaning of the word *prove*. It used to mean *test* but it has now evolved to mean something quite different. A more accurate modern version of the saying that preserved its original intent would be something like, *'the exception that challenges the rule'*.

Continuum problems

As we have seen in the example of the Sorites Paradox (with the grains of salt) or Homer Simpson's baldness, there are some cases in life where things change gradually from one state to another. Some people, however, tend to see everything in black and white, as an example of either one thing or another, and this can lead to errors. We set out some of these below.

False dichotomy

A false dichotomy is a misleading account of the available alternatives, dividing them into two when in fact there may be more options. For example, if you were to classify all people as either mods or rockers, or as upper class or working class. Both of these cases ignore the possibility that there are other options. In the first case, that there may be people who are interested in other forms of music. In the second, it ignores the possibility that people may belong to the middle classes.

Black and white thinking

This is a variation on the idea of the false dichotomy, and consists in classifying every case as an instance of one of two extremes. For instance, supposing that every person is either good or evil, and that there or no cases in between. Another example is to suppose that either you do not take any kind of drugs at all, or that you are a drug addict. In these cases there are other options between the two extremes.

In some cases black and white thinking is appropriate, but be aware when it is the case. It is appropriate if you are, say, adding up a column of figures. Here the answer is either correct or incorrect: there is no middle ground.

Drawing a line

In cases where there is a continuum, sometimes it is necessary to *draw a line* in order to distinguish one case from another. This is often done as people are growing up. We set arbitrary dates to divide people into categories, saying when they can drink, have sex, vote, drive and so on. Suppose that the law says you can drink at 18.

This doesn't mean that on your 18th birthday, you can suddenly handle your drink, whereas the day before you could not. The reason that it is done this way is that it is sensible to draw a line somewhere.

If you consider the possible alternatives – letting everyone drink including children, or prohibiting everyone from drinking no matter what their age, or assessing everybody's ability to drink on the basis of their individual merits, none are attractive. Therefore, an arbitrary line is set, even if it can seem unfair on occasion.

Slippery slope

This is another continuum problem. The idea is that if you concede that a small change to a position is acceptable it will inevitably lead to an extreme change.

For instance, some people argue against euthanasia using the slippery slope argument: that if we allow euthanasia in cases where people are terminally ill and in pain, then ultimately it will lead to the extermination of the disabled, mentally ill, the burdensome and anyone else the state or a persons relative's might consider inconvenient.

However, the slippery slope argument needs to be treated with scepticism. One should examine from empirical evidence whether in fact it applies (i.e. whether allowing a small change does lead to further undesirable changes), or whether it is possible to draw a line and make a decision that some cases will fall on one side of the line, and others on the other side.

Domino effect

The domino effect is similar to the slippery slope argument and any argument based on it should be treated with the same level of caution. It is the idea that if one thing happens then it will inevitably lead to a chain of further consequences.

The metaphor is based on the idea of a chain of dominoes standing on their ends. If one is toppled over, it will hit the next one, which will topple the next one and so on, until they have all fallen over. The domino effect was used to justify the USA's involvement in the Vietnam War.

The justification was that if Vietnam went communist then the whole of South East Asia would fall. As with the slippery slope argument, it is necessary to test the claim that such an outcome is inevitable. In the case of Vietnam, it clearly was not the case that every other country in the region became communist.

Socratic fallacy

The Socratic fallacy is the belief that if a general term cannot be defined precisely then it is not possible to identify particular cases of it. A classic example is *art*. It is notoriously difficult to find a definition of art that satisfies everyone. But it is clearly possible to identify individual cases as works of art. It is only in borderline cases that problems might arise (see *necessary and sufficient conditions and family resemblance terms*).

Vagueness

This is a related problem that we have already identified. Some concepts, such as bald, clean, loud, tall and so on, are genuinely vague. It is not clear where one crosses the line and becomes bald. This does not mean that genuine cases of baldness cannot be identified.

Causes

A common mistake is to misidentify how two separate events are related to each other by supposing that one event causes another.

Correlation equals cause confusion

This is the mistake of treating correlation as evidence of direction of causation. Events are correlated if they tend to happen together. But just because they tend to happen together does not mean that one causes the other.

For instance, there is a correlation between a person's foot size and their level of intelligence. The larger the foot size the higher the level of intelligence. This, however, does not mean that one causes the other. In fact, there is a common factor between foot size and intelligence, which is age. As you grow older your foot size increases (up to a certain age) and so does your level of intelligence.

Another example is that of a good luck charm. Suppose your football team only wins when you take a particular mascot with you. You may be superstitious and believe that there is some relation between taking it and your team winning.

In fact, this correlation is likely to be random, or possibly even non-existent. You may conveniently forget about the times you have not taken your mascot and your team has won, or those times when you have taken it and your team has lost. If there were a strict correlation, then it would be worthy of further investigation. It may be that there are *alternative explanations*.

Alternative explanations

This is a related to the correlation equals cause confusion. For example, suppose it were found that children were much more likely to be good musicians if they were brought up in a musical family. This might be used as evidence that there is a genetic component to musical ability. However, it ignores the alternative possible explanation that musical families will be more likely to bring their children up in a rich musical environment and encourage them in their musical ability. i.e. the explanation is environmental rather than genetic.

Beware that this may be open to abuse. Tobacco companies have used this strategy. In response to the suggestion that smoking tobacco causes cancer they have suggested that there is some underlying factor that means that people who are prone to cancer are for some reason more likely to be smokers. In the absence of evidence there is no reason to believe this.

Proof by ignorance

This is the mistaken supposition that, if there is no evidence for the existence of something, then it doesn't exist. For example, we have no evidence for the existence of life on other planets outside our solar system, but that does not show that there isn't any. That this approach is mistaken can be shown asking whether there is evidence for the *absence* of life outside the solar system. Since there is no conclusive evidence either way we are simply not in a position to make a decision.

Other People

Another common mistake is to examine not the strength or weakness of an argument, but instead look at who is making it, and base your conclusion on that. Whether or not an argument is a good one should be determined on its merits, not on who is making it.

Bad company fallacy

This is the mistake of attacking a position because someone who advocates it is evil, repugnant or stupid. For example, many people who oppose euthanasia cite the fact that it was practised in Nazi Germany. So, they argue that if Hitler was in favour of it, then it must be wrong.

However, Hitler's government also collected taxes and built roads. It would be absurd to argue that a government would be wrong to do either of those things on the basis that Hitler's government did them, and the same applies to the argument against euthanasia. A better arguments is needed.

Truth by authority

This is the reverse of the above position and is the similarly mistaken belief that if someone in a position of authority pronounces on a position then they must be right merely because of who they are.

Often it is sensible to believe what they say, because they may have more expertise that the layman, but the assessment should be made on the basis of the expertise, not on the person saying it. For example, if a doctor diagnoses a patient with a particular disease, it is reasonable to believe him, not on the basis of the mere fact that he is a doctor, but because that implies that he has a wealth of medical knowledge.

Universal expertise

This is a related idea and is the mistaken notion that if someone is prominent in one area then they would be equally proficient in other areas. In fact, if they are a leader in one field then it is unlikely that they will have sufficient time to gain expertise in other areas.

Continuing with the above example, although a doctor may be expert at treating patients, it does not follow that he is expert in, say, the ethics of medicine. So, he may not be qualified to say under what circumstances it would be appropriate to continue trying to save the life if a terminally ill patient in extreme pain, or the circumstances in which it would be right to allow her to die. That instead might be a job for moral philosophers, priests, politicians and the general public.

Getting personal – *ad hominem* arguments

This is another unacceptable form of argument, in that it shifts the argument away from the relevant aspect of the argument towards the person making it. For example, we have used the example of a politician who advocated compulsory state education while sending his children to a private school. While he may be open to the charge of *hypocrisy*, what he does with his children is not relevant to whether every child should be sent to a state school. So, it is not a good form of argument to attack the politician on this basis. By doing so, one is failing to address whether or not state education should be compulsory.

Another example would be that of a doctor who advocates giving up smoking and drinking, while at the same time smoking and drinking himself. The fact that he does so does not mean that his advice is incorrect. So it is not a good form of argument to say that because he smokes and drinks his advice is wrong.

'You too' arguments

This is an example of inconsistency and turns back the argument on the person making it, by showing that their argument has implications that would lead to them being inconsistent. For example, if someone were to advocate capital punishment but say at the same time saying all killing is wrong, they can be attacked because their position is inconsistent, and it is perfectly acceptable to expose this inconsistency to undermine their argument.

Truth by adage

This is the common practice of relying on a familiar statement or phrase and relying on it as a substitute for actually thinking. For instance, above we used the phrase, *'the exception that proves the rule'* and showed that as commonly used it is, in fact, wrong: the exception undermines the rule. Another example is, *'he who hesitates is lost'*. The person advancing the notion should be required to show why it is true in this case.

Onword

This concludes the section dealing with various different types of errors in reasoning. In the next section we deal with other ways of influencing people that do not rely on good argumentation, but on other ways of getting people to believe what you want them to believe.

SEVEN

RHETORICAL TECHNIQUES

Rhetorical techniques are broadly speaking the arts of persuasion. They are designed to influence people to reach a particular conclusion, but not by giving good reasons (perhaps because there aren't any). They use techniques such as assertion, emotive language and persuader words that are designed to produce a psychological effect on the person hearing them. Such techniques can be used to mask weak evidence and faulty reasoning and so you should be aware of them.

Sophistry

This is a particular form of rhetoric practised by the Sophist School in ancient Greece, and is seen in much political debate these days. Strictly, a sophist would use any technique to win an argument knowing that it was wrong, by using various dubious techniques such as begging the question, circular argument, equivocation, and various formal and informal fallacies. An example might be as follows. Consider the following conversation:

A: This cat is your mother.
B: How?
A: Is this cat yours?
B: Yes.
A: Is this cat a mother?
B: Yes.
A: Then this cat is your mother!

Rhetorical questions

This is the practice of asking a question without seeking an answer, but purely for the effect that it produces. So, for example, if you wanted to assert no one would want to live in a world with nuclear weapons, you could ask the question, 'who would want to live in such a world?' The questioner is not really seeking new information, and would probably be most unimpressed if someone were to chirp up and say, 'I would!'

Assertions

An assertion is an unsupported statement of belief made without providing any evidence to back it up. This kind of thing is seen all the time in advertising. For example, 'Buy this product and it will change you life', 'eating this protein bar will help you lose weight', and so on. Merely making the assertion does not mean that it is true. They can be persuasive however.

There are two particular types of assertion that it is important to be aware of, so that if you come across them, you can make the appropriate response: -

Research has shown that...

Quite often you will see the statement 'research has shown that …' followed by a statement designed to make you part with your money, such as '… taking this drug will reduce your chances of having a heart attack.'

If someone cites research, they should be able to state its source, so that if you wanted to, you could check on exactly what research was done, what the results were, who conducted the research, what qualifications they have, and what others in the same field thought of it.

This last is seen as particularly important with regard to scientific research. For an idea to gain acceptance it must have been subjected to what is called peer review, that is, the research must have been put before others active in the field to see what they think.

If this review is favourable then the idea may gain general acceptance. However, if an idea is particularly radical and undermines the generally accepted way of thinking (that is, the paradigm), then it may fail to gain a favourable review, even if it is true. Others in the field may have a vested interest (see below) in maintaining the status quo.

'that's a fallacy!'

This is the assertion, made in response to a line of argument, that its advocate has made an error of reasoning. So, in a debate, you might hear someone say, 'introducing capital punishment would reduce the crime rate', and in response the opponent might say, 'that's a fallacy'.

In fact, it may or may not be a fallacy, and the onus of proving that it is, is on the person making the charge. So an appropriate response is to request an explanation as to why it is a fallacy.

Emotive language

The use of emotional language is another rhetorical technique used to persuade people to think in a particular way. It can arouse emotions of approval or disapproval towards a particular person, group of people or activity. For example, an oppressive government might want to lock up their opponents, and justify doing so by calling them subversives, counter-revolutionaries or terrorists. However, those on the other side of the argument might refer to the same people as democrats, legitimate opponents or freedom fighters. In either case they are the same people and have done exactly the same thing, so unless there is some degree of agreement between the parties as to what distinguishes a legitimate opponent from a subversive, or a terrorist from a freedom fighter, then the use of such language only serves to muddy the issue.

Persuader language

Other forms of language can also be used to underpin a particular position:

Persuader words

These are words which indicate that a particular assertion is true, such as 'clearly', 'evidently', 'obviously', 'surely'. We use these all the time because if we were to have to produce evidence for every assertion we made we would die of old age. So, we assume that there are some things that are generally agreed upon and move on from there.

However, when used as a rhetorical technique, the use of these words may be dishonest. For instance, someone may assert, 'clearly, all people who commit sex crimes are mentally ill'. This may or may not be true, but it is not 'clearly' the case. The assertion needs to be backed up by evidence concerning people who commit sex crimes and what constitutes mental illness.

Also, certain words imply that a conclusion is to follow, such as 'therefore', 'so', and 'thus'. When used properly they are useful because they mark out the conclusion, but they can also be used in situations that imply a conclusion has been proved when it has not.

For instance, 'TV is a poor substitute for reading, so it should be banned'. In this case there is a suppressed premise: namely, anything that is a poor substitute for reading should be banned. This is a premise that you may or may not agree with, and it is important that such premises are made explicit.

Persuader definitions

Persuader definitions are a way of defining a term or concept in such a way that it suggests a particular conclusion, by use, say, of emotive language or by begging the question. For example, one might argue against democratic rule by defining it as 'rule by the unwashed masses'. This is designed to bias you against it by conjuring up negative connotations, but it fails to address the question of the value of democracy.

Jargon

Jargon is the use of specialist language associated with a particular profession or area of interest, and is particularly prevalent in academic, legal, scientific or technical circles. It has its uses because it can be a shorthand way of expressing a complicated idea. However, the danger of jargon is that it can be used as a means of excluding outsiders, by undermining their capacity to communicate or marking them out as different.

Pseudo – profundity

Pseudo-profundity is a way of making statements that appear to be clever, deep and meaningful, but which aren't. One way that this is done is by talking in paradoxes or by using oxymorons. For example, statements such as, 'the more you travel, the more you stay in the same place', 'the wisest people are the most stupid', and so on. In some circumstances these statements may say something interesting and profound, but it doesn't follow that they always do. They are easily made up and can a way of hiding one's ignorance on a matter.

Another way of appearing clever is to use banal statements. For instance, 'at birth we are all children'. This appears to say something profound but in fact it is completely vacuous.

A third way of attempting to appear clever is to ask rhetorical questions without attempting to provide any answers. One might ask, 'can we ever really know anyone?' or, 'is human life just a meaningless blip of existence?' To be really clever and profound, you might try answering these questions!

Newspeak and political correctness

Newspeak is a term derived from the book 1984, and is used as a way of making some thoughts impossible to think by abolishing the use of the word. For instance, all extra-marital sex is referred to as sexcrime. It is based on the controversial assumption that if there is no word for a particular concept, then it is not possible to think about that concept.

Newspeak is related to the modern concept of political correctness, which supposes that that there is a right and a wrong way to talk about certain concepts, and using the wrong terminology is ignorant, uncaring, offensive or reactionary.

The use of politically correct terminology may be appropriate as long as it is not used as a substitute for thinking. If there are good reasons for using it then this is acceptable but it can cause problems and lead to confusion.

For instance, in the USA the term African American is now generally used to refer to black people instead of calling them black. The motive for doing so is honourable as it is aimed at countering racism.

However, what should an American who is not black but whose family comes from, say, Egypt be called? Or a black person from Denmark who just happens to live in the US? Sticking rigidly to the label could wrongly categorise both of these people and possibly cause the very offence that it was seeking to avoid.

The important point is not the rightness or wrongness of using a particular phrase, but ensuring that doing so does not obscure the underlying meaning.

Distraction and irrelevance

These are ways of shifting a discussion away from the matter under discussion by taking the discussion into unrelated topics: -

The politician's answer

This is a technique that politicians use a great deal, hence its name. It is a means of avoiding giving a direct answer to a question. A politician might want to do this because a clear answer will mean that he is open to having weaknesses in his position exposed.

For example, a government minister may be asked, 'do you agree with the government's policy to go to war with Antarctica', and he replies, 'the government's policy is perfectly clear. We will go to war with them if they do not agree to certain conditions and U.N. resolutions.'

He fails to say whether he personally agrees with the policy. He may have a number of reasons for doing so. One might be that he disagrees with the war, but wants to keep his job, and giving a true answer would rock the boat leading to the possibility that he might be dismissed (see vested interests).

Another means of avoiding giving a direct answer that is used by politicians is to attack their opponents rather than justifying their own position.

Suppose that a party had been elected on a mandate not to raise taxes, but did put taxes up. If pressed on this a government minister might distract attention from this by talking about their opponents, asking whether anyone would want them running the economy instead with their 'disastrous record of economic mismanagement'. This completely detracts from the failure of the governing party to keep its promises.

No hypothetical-answers move

This is another technique much used by politicians. It is used to avoid giving difficult or inconvenient answers about what they will do in future situations. If they were to give a straight answer, they could then be held to it if that situation were to come to pass.

For example, suppose that the government had been elected on a promise not to regulate internet trade because they want to encourage internet companies from around the world to set up in their country. They are then asked whether they will regulate internet trade it if it is shown that unregulated use of the internet is beneficial to fraudsters, terrorists and pornographers.

One way a government spokesman might try to get out of answering that would be to say,

'that is a hypothetical situation. I never answer questions about hypothetical situations. Lets deal with the situation as it is here and now'.

This is a dishonest approach, because politicians answer questions that deal with hypothetical situations all the time. A hypothetical situation is any situation that does not actually exist. So any situation concerning how the future might turn out is a hypothetical situation.

All political promises that are based on what a party will do if and when they are elected deal with hypothetical situations. So, the real distinction is between hypothetical situations that politicians want to talk about, and the ones that they do not.

Red herrings

This is a way of taking the discussion onto a new tack and away from the meat of the issue. A red herring is used when interesting but irrelevant information is presented in an attempt to distract us from discussion of the matter at hand. The approach is often used in detective novels and films to try and convince the reader that someone other than the murderer may have committed the crime.

An example of how one might be used in argumentation: suppose global pollution is being discussed, and someone argues that anti-matter might be used as a source of vast amounts of clean power. This may be scientifically interesting but is irrelevant to how we might use energy policy now to clean up the world at present, because there is no prospect at all of using anti-matter as a source of power in the near or even distant future.

The straw man

The straw man is another technique designed to take the focus off the main issue by putting forward a version of one's opponent's views that is easily defeated, and using this as an argument against the meat of the opponent's position.

For instance, one might argue against the morality of democratic systems by pointing that Adolph Hitler was democratically elected and his government was the worst example of tyranny. However, this fails to deal with the merits of democratic systems in that they broadly reflect the wishes of the majority population, and ignores the specific factors in 1930s Germany that left it vulnerable to take over by extremist parties.

Shifting the goal posts

Yet another way of moving the discussion away from the issue, this happens when one changes one's views midway through the discussion to

Analytical Thinking

adopt a view that is more easily defended.

For instance, suppose that I started off by advocating that anyone who killed another person should be sentenced to life imprisonment. You might point out that this might mean doctors who accidentally killed their patients would be liable for life imprisonment. I might respond by suggesting that I only meant those who intended to kill someone else should be imprisoned.

You respond that this would include soldiers in time of war and police trying to arrest armed criminals. I then respond by suggesting that only those who intentionally kill and who are not members of the police or the armed forces should be imprisoned. I have now reached a more reasonable view, but I have shifted considerably from my original position.

Zigzagging

Zigzagging is an extreme form of shifting the goalposts, and occurs when one of the parties jumps from one topic to another without allowing any meaningful discussion to get going. This may be a way of avoiding criticism, or it may just mean that the guilty party has an extremely short attention span!

An example might go as follows:

Homer: I think that all criminals should be locked up and the key thrown away.

Lisa: But wouldn't that be unjust? Some crimes are much more serious than others.

Homer: Yeah, but the police should be allowed to carry bigger guns then they would be able to catch many more criminals.

Lisa: Wouldn't that mean more criminals would also carry bigger guns and lead to more violence?

Homer: They should use Kalashnikovs. They are really good.

Lisa: What's this got to do with how we punish criminals?

Homer: I like guns.

In addition to Homer's rather worrying liking for guns, it is impossible to engage him in argument, because he keeps changing the topic under discussion

Deception

Another way that can be used to advance one's case is to use deception. It goes without saying that the use of deception is a dishonest approach, but as we all know, it can be effective.

Lying

Lying is making as untrue statement, knowing or believing it to be untrue. The second element – that is, knowing that it the statement is untrue – is essential, otherwise the statement is simply a mistake.

Lying is generally to be avoided because it undermines the ability to communicate. If you were to lie habitually then you might assume that everyone else lies habitually, but if everyone were to lie, it would be impossible to communicate accurately.

Having said that, there are times when most people would say that it is acceptable to lie. For instance, if someone were diagnosed with a terminal disease it might be acceptable to tell them that they would not experience a great deal of pain in order to protect their feelings. Or, suppose you were at home with a friend. Suddenly, there is a banging at your door and someone carrying an axe breaks in demanding to know where your friend is (who has now by now hidden away), saying that he wants to kill him. In such a case, you might feel justified in lying to the potential axe murderer.

Economy with the truth

Being economical with the truth falls short of deliberate lying, in that it lacks the element of making an untrue statement, but it is similar in that it is involves an intention to mislead.

One does this by omitting or distorting relevant information that is clearly necessary. For instance, a policeman might ask a witness to a crime whether he saw the accused entering or leaving the house where the crime was committed. The witness might answer no, but omit to mention that he had seen him inside the house through the window. The problem with this kind of deception is that it places the onus on the interrogator to ask exactly the right question, and if they lack information, as they might, they may not know precisely what question is the right one to ask.

Onword

We have now dealt with various rhetorical techniques that can be used to mislead one's opponent. In the upcoming final section of the Analytical Thinking part of this course, we deal with various psychological factors that may affect one's ability to think clearly about a subject.

EIGHT

PSYCHOLOGICAL FACTORS

These are factors that reduce people's ability or motivation to think rationally about a situation, or which increase their incentive to be dishonest with themselves or others.

We have divided these into two categories. The first is broadly what might be called excuses. The second covers the remaining psychological factors.

Excuses

There are a number of ways that we might make excuses for our behaviour:
-

Wishful thinking

This occurs when we believe that something is true because we would like it to be true. It is often suggested that one reason for people's belief in God is wishful thinking, the reasoning being that in the absence of any evidence for a belief in God, we believe because it makes life more bearable to think that there is someone up there who is concerned about us, who loves us and who will look after us in times of trouble.

Other people might believe in aliens or ghosts, again not based on evidence, but on a wish to believe in something that makes life more meaningful. Sometimes, wishful thinking can lead us into trouble. For instance, we might think that we are capable of lifting more weight, or running further or faster than we can and as a result get injured. This is because we are more concerned with getting a particular result than with how we are going to get there.

Rationalisation

A rationalisation occurs when we disguise the real reason for our actions with a justification that allows us to do what we want to do rather than what we should do. So, for example, if we saw a wallet in the street we might pick it up and keep it, and not hand it in to the police. Our justification for keeping it is that if we didn't keep it someone else would, or that it would take too much time and energy to return it. However, this is not the real reason, which is that we just want to keep the money. The reason we give serves to mask the real reason.

Two rationalisations that are often given are: -

1   Everybody does it

This is an excuse people often offer for their own bad behaviour. For instance, people might justify driving at excessive speeds or failing to declare the full amount owing on their tax return on the basis that everyone else does it. However, it is almost certainly not the case that everyone does it, and those people that refrain from it are then at a disadvantage, because they fail to obtain the benefit obtained by cheating. In any case, just because a large number of people do something, that does not make it right.

2   It never did me any harm

This is a reason people often give for continuing with a policy that seems otherwise unjustifiable. It is often used as a justification for retaining corporal punishment in schools, offered by people who were beaten when they were children. However, it is a form of generalisation, from one case to all cases. The advocate is implying that because corporal punishment did not hurt him personally, then it cannot hurt anyone. However, this is not obviously the case. It would require empirical evidence to show it to be so.

Personal factors

Other psychological reasons that might prevent us from thinking or arguing clearly are:

Prejudice

This is a belief that is held in the absence of good evidence to back it up. An obvious example is the belief that a person may be more likely to have certain bad characteristics based purely on the colour of their skin. Another example may be the belief that a person who has been to a particular university would be suitable for a particular job. Prejudices are something we are all subject to, but it is important to become aware of them and they can be overcome by analysing the relevant evidence.

Vested interests

This occurs when we have a personal interest in achieving a particular outcome and it is these interests that determine the conclusion we arrive at, and not the merits of the case. For instance, if a politician were making a decision to buy a computer system from either Company A or Company B, since he is responsible for spending other people's money, it should be the case that he makes the decision based on proper considerations such as price, value for money, what the system is capable of, and so on. It would be unacceptable if he were to make it on the basis that he had shares in Company B and he wanted to get rich. However, the fact that someone has a vested interest does not mean that they will inevitably reach the wrong conclusion. In this case, Company B may be the right one to go with in any case.

Kowtowing

Kowtowing is a variation on the idea of universal expertise and truth by authority and is the sin of being overly deferential to a person's views purely because of who that person was or is. For instance, suppose you were a big fan of John Lennon's music, and used this as a basis for following his beliefs on radical politics and any other subjects, thinking that he was incapable of being wrong on any subject. To take one's entire belief system from someone else is intellectually lazy, gives no guarantee that you will reach the right conclusion, and is an indication of deep psychological problems.

This concludes the section on personal factors that may affect one's ability to reach an acceptable conclusion. We suggest that you now refer back to the introduction to take the steps we set out there to make sure that you are thoroughly familiar with the all the different techniques of argumentation, mistakes, rhetorical techniques and psychological factors we have identified in the Critical Thinking part of this course.

Onword

To help you to put what we have covered so far into practice, we have included an imaginary interview with two politicians. You can use this to help identify some of the different factors we have covered in this course.

NINE

PRACTICE PASSAGE

In this section is an imaginary discussion between two politicians, an interviewer and an audience. In it, we have included a number of the factors that we have covered in the Analytical Thinking course. The passage is set out twice.

In the first version, you will see just the interview and nothing else. In the second, we have annotated the passage with various instances of poor reasoning. We suggest that you work through the first passage and try to identify as many reasoning errors as you can. Then refer to the annotated passage to see how well you have done. See if you can spot any errors that we may have missed!

Passage

(I is the interviewer, A is the audience, B & C are politicians)

I: After all the talking, speculation and contradictory opinion polls, we are about to find out what the people of this nation finally think when they go to vote tomorrow. B, what do you think they will decide.
B: I have every confidence in the good sense of the people. At last they will have the opportunity to turn away from faceless capitalism and return to a more caring society. Power will return to the people. For too long it has been in the hands of those who give money to the governing party, cronies and friends of the prime minister. It's about time power returned to the people who really care about democracy.
I: C, do you agree with this?
C: No. Of course this is complete nonsense. The people are far too clever to fall for this rubbish. What they really want is a continuation of the sound and prudent economic management that we have delivered to this country.
I: Thank you. Now can we have some questions from the audience?
A: I would like to ask C if he thinks that his party's policy of cutting taxes for the rich is justifiable when there are so many poor people around.

C: As a member of the government I have to make many difficult decisions. Of course no one wants poverty and we would like to eradicate it, but it is not straightforward. We believe that the best way of removing poverty is increasing prosperity. We must keep taxes low because this will lead to a more entrepreneurial culture, which will benefit everyone.
B: That may be true but a smaller portion of government spending is being spent on overseas aid than ever before. What about the poor elsewhere in the world?
C: I believe that charity begins at home. Of course, foreign aid is important but we must look after the poor people in this country.
B: But the number of people in poverty in this country has risen. I have just seen some figures that show one in four people are now living in poverty.
C: That depends on what you mean by poverty. I have seen those figures and they include all the people who do not take foreign holidays. How ridiculous is that! Many of these people supposedly in poverty are claiming unemployment benefit while working on the side. Last week we had the case of an asylum seeker who is living in a house worth £350,000 all paid for by the taxpayer.
B: But what about the increasing number of homeless people sleeping on the streets? They are undoubtedly poor.
C: We are doing what we can, but it is no good your party proposing vast increases in public spending to deal with these problems without saying how much taxes will have to rise to pay for it.
I: That's a fair point isn't it? You have promised billions in extra expenditure, but you have not said how you are going to pay for it. You have promised not to raise taxes.
B: What worries me is how my opponent's party can justify selling off all our industries. Soon we will have to pay for the air we breathe.
I: That's not exactly what I was asking. The audience would be very interested to know if you are planning to raise income tax to pay for your promises.
B: I was just getting to that. If we do, it will be through no fault of our own but because of the shortsightedness of the current government. Not only have they privatised everything, but they have caused long-term damage to all of our public services. The state of our hospital buildings is an absolute disgrace.
C: That's just not true. We have put an enormous amount of money into our hospitals. What they need is not more money but a new management style.
B: Exactly. You want to close the hospitals down and put the dying

back on the streets unless people can afford expensive private surgery.
C: I did not say that. I said that our hospitals need reforming, and people's attitudes need to change too. Too much government interference is a bad thing. People need to learn more about how to live healthily so they can avoid hospitals in the first place. They need better education.
A: Many women are concerned about your proposals to limit the right to abortion. Don't you believe that it is a woman's right to choose what to do with her own body?
B: Yes of course, but the issue isn't quite that simple. The more fundamental issue is the right to life of all human beings. I know that some people say that an unborn child has no rights and that abortion is acceptable up to a certain time. However, you cannot just draw a line and say that after a certain time the unborn child is a living person, with all the commensurate rights, but that the previous day it was just a collection of cells. Abortion can only be justified when its purpose is to save the life of the mother and even then we must be terribly careful
A: What if the foetus is likely to be born deformed. Would you condemn it to a life of suffering?
B: That's very dangerous. If you start killing unborn children because of that then you start advocating euthanasia or infanticide on the same grounds.
I: And you, C, what do you think about this issue. How will you vote?
C: This is a very complicated issue. There are cases where I think abortion may be necessary for the sake of the mother, but the sanctity of life is an important principle. I suspect that some intermediate position is probably appropriate. We should allow it in some cases but not all of them.
I: So how would you vote on the abortion issue.
C: I think the important thing to focus on is the reasons why women feel the need to have abortions, and what drives them to such an extreme position.
I: Well, that concludes our interview. I would like to thank you very much for sharing your views with the audience.

Annotated passage

I: After all the talking, speculation and contradictory opinion polls, we are about to find out what the people of this nation finally think when they go to vote tomorrow. B, what do you think they will decide.
B: I have every confidence in the good sense of the people (*this sentence carries little meaning but intends to appeal to the audience by flattering them*). At last they will have the opportunity to turn away from faceless capitalism (*the use of the word faceless gives an emotional tone designed to produce a specific and unflattering effect*) and return to a more caring society (*the implication here is of a stark choice with no middle ground*). Power will return to the people (*this is arguably a stipulative definition because he presumably means his own party and its supporters*). For too long it has been in the hands of those who give money to the governing party, cronies and friends of the prime minister (*here he has repeated the same idea three different ways – a common way of emphasising a point, but adding nothing factual*). It's about time power returned to the people who really care about democracy (*again the word 'people' is used to refer to his party*).
I: C, do you agree with this?
C: No. Of course this is complete nonsense (*this is a mere assertion without any supporting facts*). The people are far too clever to fall for this rubbish. What they really want is a continuation of the sound and prudent economic management (*the use of the words sound and prudent is used to convey a certain effect - the same policies could equally be characterised as unimaginative and uninspired*) that we have delivered to this country.
I: Thank you. Now can we have some questions from the audience?
A: I would like to ask C if he thinks that his party's policy of cutting taxes for the rich is justifiable when there are so many poor people around.
C: As a member of the government (*this phrase is designed to indicate that he is an authority on his subject and his views are to be taken seriously*) I have to make many difficult decisions. Of course no one wants poverty and we would like to eradicate it, but it is not straightforward. We believe that the best way of removing poverty is increasing prosperity (*this phrase is circular -increasing prosperity and removing poverty are the same thing*). We must keep taxes low because this will lead to a more entrepreneurial culture, which will benefit everyone (*he has not shown the intervening steps of the argument which show how one thing leads to the other*).
B: That may be true but a smaller portion of government spending is

being spent on overseas aid than ever before. What about the poor elsewhere in the world?

C: I believe that charity begins at home (*this is an appeal to truth by adage and adds nothing to the argument*). Of course, foreign aid is important but we must look after the poor people in this country.

B: But the number of people in poverty in this country has risen. I have just seen some figures that show one in four people are now living in poverty.

C: That depends on what you mean by poverty. I have seen those figures and they include all the people who do not take foreign holidays (*here he is exploiting different ways of defining poverty*). How ridiculous is that! Many of these people supposedly in poverty are claiming unemployment benefit while working on the side. Last week we had the case of an asylum seeker who is living in a house worth £350,000 all paid for by the taxpayer (*here he is making an implied rash generalisation, implying that many 'poor' people are in fact milking the system*).

B: But what about the increasing number of homeless people sleeping on the streets? They are undoubtedly poor.

C: We are doing what we can, but it is no good your party proposing vast increases in public spending to deal with these problems without saying how much taxes will have to rise to pay for it (*here he is shifting the goalposts, by diverting attention away from his own policies and onto the policies of his opponents*).

I: That's a fair point isn't it? You have promised billions in extra expenditure, but you have not said how you are going to pay for it. You have promised not to raise taxes.

B: What worries me is how my opponent's party can justify selling off all our industries. Soon we will have to pay for the air we breathe (*here B is caricaturing C's position and using a stock phrase to convey an emotional point; he is also alluding to the possibility of a slippery slope, which of course is by no means inevitable; furthermore he is shifting the goalposts by diverting attention away from the point at issue*).

I: That's not exactly what I was asking. The audience would be very interested to know if you are planning to raise income tax to pay for your promises.

B: I was just getting to that (*this phrase is aimed at eliciting sympathy by implying that he had been interrupted - it also makes it more difficult to interrupt him in the future*). If we do, it will be through no fault of our own but because of the shortsightedness of the current government. Not only have they privatised everything, but they have caused long-term damage to all of our public services. The state of our hospital buildings is an absolute

disgrace *(he still fails to answer the question and again diverts attention by referring to the state of hospitals)*.
C: That's just not true. We have put an enormous amount of money into our hospitals. What they need is not more money but a new management style *(here C is forced to follow the diversion otherwise it looks like B is correct in his attack)*.
B: Exactly. You want to close the hospitals down and put the old and sick back on the streets unless people can afford expensive private surgery *(here his opponent's position is misrepresented and the use of emotionally toned language - old and sick - helps elicit sympathy for that position)*.
C: I did not say that. I said that our hospitals need reforming, and people's attitudes need to change too. Too much government interference is a bad thing *(this is a tautology – saying the same thing twice; too much of anything is a bad thing, otherwise it wouldn't be too much!)*. People need to learn more about how to live healthily so they can avoid hospitals in the first place. They need better education.
A: Many women are concerned about your proposals to limit the right to abortion. Don't you believe that it is a woman's right to choose what to do with her own body *(this is begging the question, by assuming that a foetus is part of a woman, when the question at issue is whether it is a separate human with its own rights)*?
B: Yes of course, but the issue isn't quite that simple. The more fundamental issue is the right to life of all human beings *(here B is also begging the question by referring to the foetus as a human being - this is the question at issue)*. I know that some people say that an unborn child has no rights and that abortion is acceptable up to a certain time. However, you cannot just draw a line and say that after a certain time the unborn child is a living person, with all the commensurate rights, but that the previous day it was just a collection of cells. Abortion can only be justified when its purpose is to save the life of the mother and even then we must be terribly careful
A: What if the foetus *(A, who is in favour of abortion, uses the word foetus, which elicits less emotional sympathy)* is likely to be born deformed. Would you condemn it to a life of suffering?
B: That's very dangerous. If you start killing unborn children because of that then you start advocating euthanasia or infanticide on the same grounds *(here B uses a slippery slope argument. He does not establish why allowing abortion leads to these other actions)*.
I: And you, C, what do you think about this issue. How will you vote?
C: This is a very complicated issue. There are cases where I think

abortion may be necessary for the sake of the mother, but the sanctity of life is an important principle. I suspect that some intermediate position is probably appropriate (*C tries to sound detached and dispassionate. However, he is probably trying to avoid giving an answer because both positions are controversial*). We should allow it in some cases but not all of them.

I: So how would you vote on the abortion issue.

C: I think the important thing to focus on is the reasons why women feel the need to have abortions, and what drives them to such an extreme position (*again, he tries to take an intermediate position here without taking a stand*).

I: Well, that concludes our interview. I would like to thank you very much for sharing your views with the audience.

Onword

This completes the first part of the course. The following section is Logical Thinking Problems. Here we have set out a number of pure logical problems which should enhance your abilities to think clearly.

Analytical Thinking

LOGICAL THINKING PROBLEMS

Write the answers in the spaces provided. If you are not sure how to answer them, look at the answers to the first few questions and see if you can work out how they are arrived at. The questions get progressively harder and more bizarre. Answers are on page 91.

1.   Babies are illogical.
Nobody is despised who can manage a crocodile.
Illogical persons are despised.
Answer:

2.   My saucepans are the only things that I have that are made of tin.
I find all your presents very useful.
None of my saucepans are of the slightest use.
Answer:

3.   No potatoes of mine, that are new, have been boiled.
All of my potatoes in this dish are fit to eat.
No unboiled potatoes of mine are fit to eat.
Answer:

4.   No ducks waltz.
No officers ever decline to waltz.
All my poultry are ducks.
Answer:

5.   Everyone who is sane can do logic.
No lunatics are fit to serve on a jury.
None of your sons can do logic.
Answer:

6.   There are no pencils of mine in this box.
No sugarplums of mine are cigars.
The whole of my property that is not in the box, consists of cigars.
Answer:

7.	No experienced person is incompetent.
Jenkins is always blundering.
No competent person is always blundering.
Answer:

8.	No terriers wander among the signs of the zodiac.
Nothing that does not wander among the signs of the zodiac is a comet.
Nothing but a terrier has a curly tail.
Answer:

9.	No one takes the Times newspaper, unless he is well educated.
No hedgehogs can read.
Those who cannot read are not well educated.
Answer:

10.	All puddings are nice.
This dish is a pudding.
No nice things are wholesome.
Answer:

11.	My gardener is well worth listening to on military subjects.
No one can remember the battle of Waterloo, unless he is very old.
Nobody is really worth listening to on military subjects, unless he can remember the battle of Waterloo.
Answer:

12.	All humming birds are richly coloured.
No large birds live on honey.
Birds that do not live on honey are dull in colour.
Answer:

13.	All ducks in this village that are branded 'B' belong to Mrs Bond.
Ducks in this village never wear lace collars, unless they are branded 'B'.
Mrs Bond has no grey ducks in this village.
Answer:

14.	All the old articles in this cupboard are cracked.
No jug in this cupboard is new.
Nothing in this cupboard, that is cracked, will hold water.

Analytical Thinking

Answer:

15. All unripe fruit is unwholesome.
All these apples are wholesome.
No fruit, grown in the shade, is ripe.
Answer:

16. Puppies, that will not lie still, are always grateful for the loan of a skipping-rope.
A lame puppy would not say 'thank you' if you offered to lend it a skipping-rope.
None but lame puppies ever care to do worsted-work.
Answer:

17. No name in this list is unsuitable for the hero of a romance.
Names beginning with a vowel are always melodious.
No name is suitable for a hero of a romance, if it begins with a consonant.
Answer:

18. All members of the House of Commons have perfect self-command.
No M.P., who wears a coronet, should ride in a donkey-race.
All members of the House of Lords wear coronets.
Answer:

19. No goods in this shop that have been bought and paid for are still on sale.
None of the goods may be carried away, unless labelled 'sold'.
None of the goods are labelled 'sold' unless they have been bought and paid for.
Answer:

20. No acrobatic feats, that are not announced in the bills of a circus, are ever attempted there.
No acrobatic feat is possible, if it involves turning a quadruple somersault.
No impossible acrobatic feat is ever announced in a circus bill.
Answer:

21. Nobody, who really appreciates Beethoven, fails to keep silence while the Moonlight-Sonata is being played.

Guinea pigs are hopelessly ignorant of music.
No one, who is hopelessly ignorant of music, ever keeps silence while the Moonlight-Sonata is being played.
Answer:

22.   Coloured flowers are always scented.
I dislike flowers that are not grown in the open air.
No flowers grown in the open air are colourless.
Answer:

23.   Showy talkers think too much of themselves.
No really well informed people are bad company.
People who think too much of themselves are not good company.
Answer:

24.   No boys under 12 are admitted to this school as boarders.
All the industrious boys have red hair.
None of the dayboys learn Greek.
None but those under 12 are idle.
Answer:

25.   The only articles of food that my doctor allows me are such as are not very rich.
Nothing that agrees with me is unsuitable for supper.
Wedding-cake is always very rich.
My doctor allows me all articles of food that are suitable for supper.
Answer:

26.   No discussions in our debating club are likely to rouse the British Lion, so long as they are checked when they become too noisy.
Discussions, unwisely conducted, endanger the peacefulness of our debating club.
Discussions, that go on while Tompkins is in the Chair, are likely to rouse the British Lion.
Discussions in our debating club, when wisely conducted, are always checked when they become too noisy.
Answer:

27.   All my sons are slim.
No child of mine is healthy who takes no exercise.

Analytical Thinking

All gluttons, who are children of mine, are fat.
No daughter of mine takes any exercise.
Answer:

28.   Things sold in the street are of no great value.
Nothing but rubbish can be sold for a song.
Eggs of the Great Auk are very valuable.
It is only what is sold in the streets that is really rubbish.
Answer:

29.   No books sold here have gilt edges, except what are in the front shop.
All the authorised editions have red labels.
All the books with red labels are priced at £5 and upwards.
None but authorized editions are ever placed in the front shop.
Answer:

30.   Remedies for bleeding, which fail to check it, are a mockery.
Tincture of Calendula is not to be despised.
Remedies, which will check the bleeding when you cut your finger, are useful.
All mock remedies for bleeding are despicable.
Answer:

31.   None of the unnoticed things, met with at sea, are mermaids.
Things entered in the log, as met with at sea, are sure to be worth remembering.
I have never met with anything worth remembering, when on a voyage.
Things met with at sea, that are noticed, are sure to be recorded in the log.
Answer:

32.   The only books in this library, that I do not recommend for reading, are unhealthy in tone.
The bound books are all well written.
All the romances are healthy in tone.
I do not recommend that you read any of the unbound books.
Answer:

33.   No birds, except ostriches, are nine feet high.
There are no birds in this aviary that belong to anyone but me.

No ostrich lives on mince pies.
I have no birds less than nine feet high.
Answer:

34.	A plum pudding, that is not really solid, is mere porridge.
Every plum pudding, served at my table, has been boiled in a cloth.
A plum pudding that is mere porridge is indistinguishable from soup.
No plum puddings are really solid, except what are served at my table.
Answer:

35.	No interesting poems are unpopular among people of real taste.
No modern poetry is free from affectation.
All your poems are on the subject of soap bubbles.
No affected poetry is popular among people of real taste.
No ancient poem is on the subject of soap bubbles.
Answer:

36.	All the fruit at this show, that fails to get a prize, is the property of the committee.
None of my peaches have got prizes.
None of the fruit, sold off in the evening, is unripe.
None of the ripe fruit has been grown in a hothouse.
All fruit that belongs to the committee is sold off in the evening.
Answer:

37.	Promise-breakers are untrustworthy.
Wine-drinkers are very communicative.
A man who keeps his promises is honest.
No teetotallers are pawnbrokers.
One can always trust a very communicative person.
Answer:

38.	No kitten that loves fish is unteachable.
No kitten without a tail will play with a gorilla.
Kittens with whiskers always love fish.
No teachable kitten has green eyes.
No kittens have tails unless they have whiskers.
Answer:

39.	All the Eton men in this college play cricket.
None but the scholars dine at the higher table.

None of the cricketers row.
My friends in this college all come from Eton.
All the scholars are rowing men.
Answer:

40. There is no box of mine here that I dare open.
My writing desk is made of rosewood.
All my boxes are painted, except what are here.
There is no box of mine that I dare not open, unless it is full of live scorpions.
All my rosewood boxes are unpainted.
Answer:

41. All writers, who understand human nature, are clever.
No one is a true poet unless he can stir the hearts of men.
Shakespeare wrote 'Hamlet'.
No writer, who does not understand human nature, can stir the hearts of men.
None but a true poet could have written 'Hamlet'.
Answer:

42. I despise anything that cannot be used as a bridge.
Everything that is worth writing an ode to would be a welcome gift to me.
A rainbow will not bear the weight of a wheelbarrow.
Whatever can be used as a bridge will bear the weight of a wheelbarrow.
I would not take as a gift things I despise.
Answer:

43. When I work a logic example without grumbling, you may be sure it is one that I can understand.
These Sorites examples are not arranged in regular order, like the examples I am used to.
No easy example ever makes my head ache.
I can't understand examples that are not arranged in regular order, like those I am used to.
I never grumble at an example, unless it gives me a headache.
Answer:

44. Every idea of mine that cannot be expressed as a syllogism is really ridiculous.

None of my ideas about Bath-buns are worth writing down.
No idea of mine, that fails to come true, can be expressed as a syllogism.
I never have any really ridiculous idea that I do not at once refer to my solicitor.
My dreams are all about Bath-buns.
I never refer any idea of mine to my solicitor, unless it is worth writing down.
Answer:

45.   None of the pictures here, except the battle-pieces, are valuable.
None of the unframed ones are varnished.
All the battle-pieces are painted in oils.
All those that have been sold are valuable.
All the English ones are varnished.
All those in frames have been sold.
Answer:

46.   Animals that do not kick are always unexcitable.
Donkeys have no horns.
A buffalo can always toss one over a gate.
No animals that kick are easy to swallow.
No hornless animal can toss one over a gate.
All animals are excitable, except buffaloes.
Answer:

47.   No one, who is going to a party, ever fails to brush his hair.
No one looks fascinating, if he is untidy.
Opium-eaters have no self-command.
Everyone, who has brushed hair, looks fascinating.
No one wears white kid gloves, unless he is going to a party.
A man is always untidy, if he has no self-command.
Answer:

48.   No husband, who is always giving his wife new dresses, can be a cross-grained man.
A methodical husband always comes home for his tea.
No one, who hangs up his hat on the gas jet, can be a man that is kept in proper order by his wife.
A good husband is always giving his wife new dresses.
No husband can fail to be cross-grained, if his wife does not keep him in

Analytical Thinking

proper order.
An unmethodical husband always hangs up his hat on the gas jet.
Answer:

49. Everything, not absolutely ugly, may be kept in a drawing room.
Nothing that is encrusted with salt is ever quite dry.
Nothing should be kept in a drawing room, unless it is free from damp.
Bathing machines are always kept near the sea.
Nothing that is made with mother-of-pearl can be absolutely ugly.
Whatever is kept near the sea gets encrusted with salt.
Answer:

50. I call no day 'unlucky' when Robinson is civil to me.
Wednesdays are always cloudy.
When people take umbrellas, the day never turns out fine.
The only days when Robinson is uncivil to me are Wednesdays.
Everybody takes his umbrella with him when it is raining.
My 'lucky' days always turn out fine.
Answer:

51. No shark ever doubts that it is well fitted out.
A fish that cannot dance a minuet is contemptible.
No fish is quite certain that it is well fitted out, unless it has three rows of teeth.
All fishes, except sharks, are kind to children.
No heavy fish can dance a minuet.
A fish with three rows of teeth is not to be despised.
Answer:

52. The entire human race, except my footmen, has a certain amount of common sense.
No one, who lives on barley sugar, can be anything but a mere baby.
None but a hopscotch player knows what real happiness is.
No mere baby has a grain of common sense.
No engine driver ever plays hopscotch.
No footman of mine is ignorant of what true happiness is.
Answer:

53. I trust every animal that belongs to me.
Dogs gnaw bones.

I admit no animals into my study, unless they will beg when told to do so.
All the animals in the yard are mine.
I admit every animal that I trust into my study.
The only animals, that are really willing to beg when told to do so, are dogs.
Answer:

54.   Animals are always mortally offended if I fail to notice them.
The only animals that belong to me are in the field.
No animal can guess a conundrum, unless it has been properly trained in a Board School.
None of the animals in the field are badgers.
When an animal is mortally offended, it always rushes about wildly and howls.
I never notice any animal, unless it belongs to me.
No animal that has been properly trained in a Board School ever rushes about wildly and howls.
Answer:

55.   I never put a cheque, received by me, on that file unless I am anxious about it.
All the cheques received by me, that are not marked with cross, are payable to the bearer.
None of them are ever brought back to me, unless they have been dishonoured at the bank.
All of them that are marked with a cross are for amounts of over £100.
All of them that are not on that file are marked 'not negotiable'.
No cheque of yours, received by me, has ever been dishonoured.
I am never anxious about a cheque, received by me, unless it should happen to be brought back to me.
None of the cheques received by me that are marked 'not negotiable' are for amounts over £100.
Answer:

56.   All the dated letters in this room are written on blue paper.
None of them are in black ink, except those that are written in the third person.
I have not filed any of them that I can read.
None of them that are written on one sheet are undated.
All of them, that are not crossed, are in black ink.

All of them, written by Brown, begin with 'Dear Sir'.
All of them, written on blue paper, are filed.
None of them, written on more than one sheet, are crossed.
None of them that begin with 'Dear Sir' are written in the third person.
Answer:

57. The only animals in this house are cats.
Every animal that is suitable for a pet loves to gaze at the moon.
When I detest an animal, I avoid it.
No animals are carnivorous, unless they prowl at night.
No cat fails to kill mice.
No animals ever take to me, except what are in this house.
Kangaroos are not suitable for pets.
None but carnivores kill mice.
I detest animals that do not take to me.
Animals, that prowl at night, always love to gaze at the moon.
Answer:

Answers

1. Babies cannot manage crocodiles
2. Your presents to me are not made of tin.
3. All my potatoes in this dish are old ones.
4. My poultry are not officers.
5. None of your sons are fit to serve on a jury.
6. No pencils of mine are sugarplums.
7. Jenkins is inexperienced.
8. No comet has a curly tail.
9. No hedgehog takes in the Times.
10. This dish is unwholesome.
11. My gardener is very old.
12. All humming-birds are small
13. No grey ducks in this village wear lace collars.
14. No jug in the cupboard will hold water.
15. These apples were grown in the sun.
16. Puppies, that will not lie still, never care to do worsted-work.
17. No name in this list is unmelodious.
18. No M.P. should ride in donkey-race, unless he has perfect self-command.
19. No goods in this shop that are still on sale may be carried away.
20. No acrobatic feat, which involves turning a quadruple somersault, is ever attempted in a circus.
21. Guinea pigs never really appreciate Beethoven.
22. No scentless flowers please me.
23. Showy talkers are not really well informed.
24. None but red-haired boys learn Greek in this school.
25. Wedding-cake always disagrees with me.
26. Discussions, that go on while Tompkins is in the chair, endanger the peacefulness of our Debating-Club.
27. All gluttons, who are children of mine, are unhealthy.
28. An egg of the Great Auk is not to be had for a song.
29. No books sold here have gilt edges, unless they are priced at £5 and upwards.
30. When you cut your finger, you will find Tincture of Calendula useful.
31. I have never come across a mermaid at sea.
32. All the romances in this library are well written.
33. No bird in this aviary lives on mince pies.

34. No plum pudding that has not been boiled in a cloth can be distinguished from soup.
35. All your poems are uninteresting.
36. None of my peaches have been grown in a hothouse.
37. No pawnbroker is dishonest.
38. No kitten with green eyes will play with a gorilla.
39. All my friends dine at the lower table.
40. My writing desk is full of live scorpions.
41. Shakespeare was clever.
42. Rainbows are not worth writing odes to.
43. These Sorties examples are difficult.
44. All my dreams come true.
45. All the English pictures here are painted in oils.
46. Donkeys are not easy to swallow.
47. Opium-eaters never wear white kid gloves.
48. A good husband always comes home for his tea.
49. Bathing machines are never made of mother-of-pearl.
50. Rainy days are always cloudy.
51. No heavy fish is unkind to children.
52. No engine driver lives on barley sugar.
53. All the animals in the yard gnaw bones.
54. No badger can guess a conundrum.
55. No cheque of yours, received by me, is payable to order.
56. I cannot read any of Brown's letters.
57. I always avoid a kangaroo.

END WORD

This concludes the Logical Thinking Course. Ensure that you continue to practise and develop your skills in the manner we have outlined in the introduction. As you start to master all of the logical techniques we have outlined in this course, you should notice a profound increase in the power of your logical and critical thinking abilities.

More Quick Courses Coming Soon!

Visualisation

Analytical Thinking

Creative Thinking

Setting and Achieving Goals

Powerful States of Mind

Essential Communication Skills

Emulating Success

Healthy Eating

Healthy Sleep

Printed in Great Britain
by Amazon